EVERY PASTOR'S
FIRST 180 DAYS

EVERY PASTOR'S
FIRST 180 DAYS

*How to Start and Stay Strong
in a New Church Role*

CHARLES STONE

EQUIP PRESS

Colorado Springs

EVERY PASTOR'S
FIRST 180 DAYS

Published by Equip Press, Colorado Springs, CO

First Edition: 2019
Every Pastor's First 180 Days / Charles Stone
Paperback ISBN: 978-1-946453-91-4
eBook ISBN: 978-1-946453-92-1

EQUIP PRESS
Colorado Springs

"We spend most of our day helping churches find their next Pastor. It's so good to see that someone is now addressing what to do once you hire the new team member. In our estimation, onboarding is one of the keys to success of a new team member, and Charles has done a marvelous job of addressing the issues central to onboarding success. If you're planning on hiring in the days to come, get this book today!"

William Vanderbloemen,
Founder & CEO, Vanderbloemen

"I wish I had this book when I was a pastor. I wish all new pastors would read this book. I wish **all** pastors would read this book. It's just that good. Charles Stone guides you through the first six months of pastoral ministry. The information is gold, and the application is powerfully relevant. I now have a new book of must-reads for pastors."

Thom Rainer, Founder and CEO Church Answers,
Author of *I Am a Church Member*

CONTENTS

INTRODUCTION

The will to win is not nearly so important as the will to prepare to win.
— Vince Lombardi

⌒

Thriving in a new job or a new ministry setting challenges even the best pastor-leaders, especially in the first few months. Business statistics bear this out. One study of 20,000 executive searches revealed that 40 percent of executives hired at the senior level are pushed out, fail, or quit within 18 months.[1] So at least in the business world, the early days present unique challenges.

But are the statistics that dismal for church ministry?

Fortunately, no. Research from 1500 pastors by Lifeway Research indicated that an estimated 13 percent of senior pastors in 2005 had left the pastorate ten years later for reasons other than death or retirement.[2] At the same time, pastors aren't quitting in droves, they still face considerable stress, as the average pastoral tenure is between three and four years.[3] That same survey revealed these realities.

---

1   anon., "Executive Search - A Broken Model," accessed May 21, 2019, http://lumenispartners.com/a-broken-model/.

2   "Despite Stresses, Few Pastors Give Up on Ministry," LifeWay Research, September 2015, http://www.lifewayresearch.com/2015/09/01/despite-stresses-few-pastors-give-up-on-ministry/.

3   "The Dangerous Third Year of Pastoral Tenure," ThomRainer.com, June 18, 2014, http://thomrainer.com/2014/06/dangerous-third-year-pastoral-tenure/.

- *84 percent say they're on call 24 hours a day.*
- *80 percent expect conflict in their church.*
- *54 percent find the role of pastor frequently overwhelming.*
- *53 percent are often concerned about their family's financial security.*
- *48 percent often feel the demands of ministry are more than they can handle.*
- *21 percent say their church has unrealistic expectations of them.*

Another study of over 3,700 clergy from Australia, England, and New Zealand indicated that although 86 percent were satisfied in ministry, 35 percent reported that they felt drained in fulfilling their roles.[4]

That's why I wrote *Every Pastor's First 180 Days*. I want to help pastors and ministry leaders coming to a new church (or even beginning a new phase of ministry in their existing church) thrive even in the midst of ministry stress and challenges. And thriving largely depends on understanding a critical concept that research indicates helps new leaders get off to a good start and avoid needless pain and conflict.

So whether you are a rookie or a veteran senior pastor, missionary, youth pastor, associate pastor, worship pastor, or recent seminary grad going into a new ministry setting, *Every Pastor's First 180 Days* is for you. And if you are hiring and want your new hires to succeed, *Every Pastor's First 180 Days* can help them navigate their first few months well.

Is This the Key to Early Success in a New Church or Ministry Role?

As a pastor for almost four decades, I've experienced my share of difficult starts. I've served as an associate pastor, a singles' pastor, a church planter, a teaching pastor, and a lead pastor in three churches. During each of these transitions, the new opportunity whetted my desire to make a Kingdom impact. I wanted to (and often did) jump in, share my vision, and

---

4   Mandy Robbins Leslie J. Francis, "Psychological Type and Work-Related Psychological Health among Clergy in Australia, England and New Zealand," *Journal of Psychology and Christianity* 28 (2009).

immediately change things to make what I thought would be a quick and lasting difference for the Kingdom. Yet I spent very little time, energy, and effort to plan *how* I would successfully transition in the new role to make the impact I desired. And seminary hadn't taught me what to do first in a new ministry setting.

I gave little intentional thought to what I should do those first few months, until my most recent move. I took the lead pastor role at a church in Canada after serving my entire thirty-three years of ministry life in the United States. The first five-and-a-half years (at the time of this writing) have been quite remarkable. We've grown significantly in attendance, baptisms, volunteerism, and giving. I believe the insight I share in this book helped make my transition fulfilling and successful. I'm convinced that insight can do the same for you.

I weave the story about how I applied a fundamental concept that made the difference. In the business world, it's called *onboarding*, what leaders should do in the first few months in a new job to get a good start. Although hundreds of ministry books deal with building healthy families, growing leadership skills, and improving preaching, little is written about how onboarding can make or break a ministry. I only know of a handful.

So what is onboarding? It's much more than an orientation program when a new pastor gets the manual on how to operate the copier, takes a facilities tour, and attends a meet-and-greet with volunteers. Rather, it's an intentional multi-month process of assimilation, alignment, and acquiring new tools that a new pastor must prioritize as he or she enters a new ministry role. It begins *before* the first day on the job and lasts several months. It provides a trajectory that can largely determine the direction your ministry takes for the next several years, just as a rocket's initial trajectory can determine the success of its mission. Setting a healthy trajectory will accelerate the process by which you earn social capital so that you can make long-lasting changes with Kingdom impact.[5]

---

5   T. Scott Daniels, *The First 100 Days: A Pastor's Guide* (Kansas City: Beacon Hill Press, 2011), p. 7.

The Bible often talks about planning, and onboarding is a specific kind of planning. Jesus talked about thinking ahead and planning in Luke 14:28–33 when he used the metaphors of building a tower or going to war. Throughout the Old Testament, we find examples of planning, and the book of Proverbs often counsels us to plan well (Prov 21:5; 24:27).

Onboarding reflects the truth in the adage, "You never have a second chance to make a good first impression." Undoing a wrong impression is harder than creating a good one. When people create opinions about us, they tend to stick, whether good or bad. Research even confirms what common sense has already told us: first impressions really do matter.[6] Research also confirms that effective onboarding will increase a leader's success in a new position.[7] Michael Watkins, author of one of the best business books on onboarding, *Your First 90 Days*, writes this about a leader's initial transition into a new role.

> *When I surveyed more than thirteen hundred senior HR leaders, almost ninety percent agreed that "transitions into new roles are the most challenging times in the professional lives of leaders." And nearly three-quarters agreed that "success or failure during the first few months is a strong predictor of overall success or failure in the job." So even though a bad transition does not necessarily doom you to failure, it makes success a lot less likely.[8]*

---

6   Robert B. Lount, et al., "Getting off on the Wrong Foot: The Timing of a Breach and the Restoration of Trust," *Personality & Social Psychology Bulletin* 34, no. 12 (December 2008): 1601–12, https://doi.org/10.1177/0146167208324512.

7   Ray Williams, "Onboarding Increases Probability of Leaders' Success," Financial Post, February 5, 2010, http://business.financialpost.com/2010/05/02/onboarding-increases-probability-of-leaders-success/.

8   Michael D. Watkins, *The First 90 Days: Proven Strategies for Getting Up to Speed Faster and Smarter, Updated and Expanded*, (Boston, Massachusetts: Harvard Business Review Press, 2013), p. 1.

Watkins also wisely notes that it takes time for a new leader to move from being a consumer of the organization's resources to being a value producer. He calls this point the *break-even point*. His survey of two hundred company CEOs and presidents revealed that they estimated it takes a new hire six months to cross that break-even point.[9] Thus, I suggest that a new pastor create a six-month onboarding plan reflected in the book's title, *Every Pastor's First 180 Days*.

Most business onboarding books generally target the first ninety to one hundred days, a timeframe traced back to Napoleon Bonaparte. It took him 111 days to return from exile, reinstate himself as France's ruler, and wage war against the Prussian and English army. And President Franklin Roosevelt's achievements in the first one hundred days after he became president helped cement the one-hundred-day window as a common time frame. In his efforts to ease the Great Depression, he effected significant change in those first one hundred days, pushing fifteen major bills through Congress. Such radical change is seldom wise for a pastor during his first few months, unless the 'ship is sinking.' Roosevelt's example simply provides a suggested window for intentional transition, especially in the business and government arena.

However, a church is different from a business or the government. Churches often move slower. So I recommend double the time frame that most onboarding business experts suggest. Six months is an initial planning horizon. You'll create many more plans afterward, but this initial window provides a reasonable time frame from which to start. There's nothing hallowed about six months, and you may find that a four-month onboarding process suits your new ministry. You may also find that it takes longer. Your unique culture will determine the pace.

I served in the U.S. for thirty-three years before I took my lead pastor role in Canada. I'm learning that change in a Canadian church culture takes more time than change in a U.S. church culture. And although I've built the concepts around six months, you can adapt my concepts to the time frame that fits your unique setting.

---

9   ibid, p. 3 .

So if you are a pastoral leader about to begin a new role, *Every Pastor's First 180 Days* is for you. And if you are a lead pastor or an executive pastor and plan to hire new ministry leaders, I suggest making this book required reading for your new hires. I believe what they learn will help them transition more successfully to make the greatest Kingdom impact. It will help them avoid digging deep holes from which they'll spend unnecessary energy to overcome (and keep you from expending your energy to pull them out).

An Overview of the Book

You'll notice that I weave insight about the brain into many chapters. God created this magnificent three-pound powerhouse, and the Scriptures refer to the mind over 160 times. I believe the more we understand how our brains and minds function, the better we will do life and leadership. I believe this so much that I wrote a book on the subject, *Brain Savvy Leaders: The Science of Significant Ministry.*

I've used two acronyms, *PALM* and *SADDLE,* as visual metaphors to help you retain and recall the key principles of onboarding. Since up to one-half of our brain is dedicated in some way to visual processing,[10] pictures stick better in our minds. The saying, "A picture is worth a thousand words," has a solid scientific basis. That's why I've used these visuals.

I've divided the book into three sections. In *Section I,* I focus on four core principles that provide a foundation for successful onboarding, represented by *PALM.* They embody four practices that not only make a transition run smoother but represent leadership priorities I recommend every good leader embrace whether or not they are new to a ministry. Leaders should practice these regularly. I briefly explain *PALM* below, with the corresponding chapter number and a summary.

---

10   anon., "MIT Research - Brain Processing of Visual Information," Brain Processing of
      Visual Information, December 19, 1996, http://news.mit.edu/1996/visualprocessing.

Prioritize self and family care (chapter 1)

In this chapter, you'll learn about four key areas that impact your family and your emotional, spiritual, and physical self. You'll also learn specific ways to keep these healthy and balanced, especially in the beginning of a new ministry.

Avidly overcommunicate (chapter 2a)

In the first part of this chapter, I'll explain why we need to overcommunicate and how doing so helps moderate the fear circuits in the brains of the people in our ministries, thus making them more open to change. I also share specific ways I overcommunicated to encourage you to develop your own communication plan.

Listen and learn (chapter 2b)

I combine both avidly overcommunicate and listen and learn into one chapter because they represent two sides of the same coin— one takes in (listening) and the other gives out (communicating). By emphasizing how listening improves leadership, in this chapter, you'll grasp the power of a listening ear and understand brain insight about listening. You'll see that by listening and communicating, you are listening and can help move your church or ministry in the direction you believe God is leading you.

Manage change wisely (chapter 3)

You'll glean key insights about change management that work. I'll share specific steps I took to manage change to illustrate options that can help you manage change in your situation. In this chapter, I also include neuroscience insights that affect change.

In *Section II*, I suggest a specific six-step process to use during the first six months of your new ministry. I use the acronym SADDLE to describe this process. I'm not particularly fond of horses, but I know that to ride a horse effectively, you need a saddle. John Wayne, the famous Hollywood actor who appeared in eighty-four westerns, once said, "Courage is being scared to death—but saddling up anyway." Onboarding can be scary, but the better we prepare for it, the more successful we'll be. Every ministry (horse) is different, and the SADDLE plan helps you design your plan (your saddle) to fit your unique ministry setting.

To help you implement the SADDLE plan, I've created several tools you can download at the book's bonus tools web page. Each time you see this symbol, ∞, it denotes a downloadable tool organized by chapter available at the website at www.charlesstone.com/freebies. Here's an overview of the SADDLE plan:

Start Early (chapter 4)

In this chapter, I'll explain how starting early, even before your first day on the job, can prepare you for a successful transition. I'll also suggest other steps to take before day one.

Avoid Common Pitfalls (chapter 5)

You'll learn the seven common pitfalls pastors often make in a new ministry setting. I will share where I was successful and where I succumbed to some of those pitfalls.

Define Reality (chapter 6)

By highlighting some surprising issues, I discovered at my new church, you'll identify with some surprises you may face in your new setting. You'll learn about these subsurface, simmering issues that, had I missed them, would have considerably slowed the forward progress we made during the first few months.

Develop a Game Plan (chapter 7)

In this chapter, I'll share my six-month game plan and how I developed it. You'll learn the steps necessary to create your own game plan for your first six months. I will also explain the value of creating a storyline about yourself and share the storyline I intentionally tried to create about myself.

Lead Your Team (chapter 8)

I share specific decisions I made with my key leaders that made a positive difference. You'll discover why you should focus on team building and how to do it. I will also share some key insights I learned about leading in Canada that differ from leading in the U.S. yet may be applicable in church settings in other countries outside of North America.

Establish Trust (chapter 9)

I explain why I prioritized building trust with our leaders and why I believe new pastors should do the same with theirs. You'll learn some brain-based insights on how to build genuine trust with your team, whether they're paid staff or volunteer leaders.

In Section III, I close with a final chapter (chapter 10) called Pulling It All Together to help you keep your plan on track during the first six months. I encourage you to take thirty minutes each week, fifteen minutes at the beginning of your week and fifteen minutes at the end of your week, to plan and evaluate, respectively, your onboarding. More time is better, but thirty minutes is the minimum. To facilitate this, I provide twenty-six weekly onboarding exercises that include key questions, a key principle to review, and prompts about next steps. In that chapter, I explain how to do this and provide the twenty-six exercises as a complete download. ∞ I then wrap things up with some final thoughts and list and describe each tool that is downloadable from the website.

I begin each chapter with an interesting quote that applies to the content and then give a snapshot that summarizes the chapter. At the end of some chapters, I include brief insights about onboarding from a current or former executive pastor of a large church. I've asked some of the most respected executive pastors in North America to share suggestions about successful onboarding and to share things we should avoid that they've observed in new hires. I conclude each chapter with a "pause and reflect" question and a suggested Next-step application to help deepen the chapter's insights. Throughout the book, I share examples of what I did right and what I did wrong during my six-month onboarding process.

My Story

I've lived in the U.S. my entire life and served in five different churches during my first thirty-three years as a pastor. In my last role in the U.S., I served as lead pastor in a church of eleven hundred in the Chicago suburbs. Toward the end of those seven-and-a-half years, I began to sense God's stirring in my heart for something new. After a good run at that church, I stepped aside to focus on some other goals I couldn't accomplish if I continued serving full-time as a lead pastor.

So from April 2012 through October 2013, I no longer worked in a local church in a paid capacity. In 2012, we moved about an hour and a half away from Chicago and joined a local church where I served on a volunteer basis. We moved into a fifty-year-old house on a small lake and thoroughly enjoyed lake life. During that year and a half, I started a church coaching/ consulting ministry and an animation company, traveled internationally training pastors, wrote two books, and enjoyed a relatively pressure-free season not serving on a church staff. However, I knew that after a short season, I would return as a senior pastor. I assumed it would be in the U.S., but God had other plans.

Just before we left our church in the Chicago area, a significant church in the southeast interviewed us. We visited that church one weekend, excited about the possibility of living closer to our families who live in the south. After a weekend there, however, we realized we weren't a fit and declined the opportunity.

About a year later, four churches began conversations with us, all at the same time. One was a church in Canada that had posted their lead pastor search on the web. Here's how the ad read:

> *WestPark Church, located in northwest London, Ontario, Canada, is seeking a Lead Pastor to head our ministry team of ten professional and four support staff members. The man applying for this position will possess a contagious passion for the Word of God and be able to build, lead, and maintain a strong ministry staff with a transparent leadership style that empowers teams and encourages participation. He will champion the pursuit of our mission to "lead people on a life-changing journey."*
>
> *Our church is situated in a new subdivision development in a six-year-old, spacious, multi-functional facility of 50,000 sq. ft. on 20 acres of land with a 750 theatre-seat auditorium, a full-size gymnasium, an intimate chapel, and two separate dedicated areas designed specifically for children and students. We have an average Sunday attendance of just under 700 people, and more than 300 adults meet weekly or bi-weekly in our home LifeGroups.*

When I read the ad I thought, "Wow, this looks incredible...a good-sized church...a growing area...a fantastic facility...a commitment to small groups...team focused. Sounds like a perfect match for me." The only problem was one small word, *Canada*. I did not want to move to Canada. I was an American. I had never considered moving out of the U.S., where I had lived my entire life. It's really cold in Canada and I like warm weather. It snows a lot in Canada. Moose run around everywhere in Canada (which reflected my prejudiced view; it's not true). I don't play hockey and everybody in Canada does (they don't). I considered multiple excuses to dismiss WestPark. It wasn't until several weeks after I saw the posting and after much prayer and dialogue with my wife that I reluctantly submitted my resume.

Well, the rest is history. After several phone conversations and two visits, we knew God wanted us to move there. It's been an incredibly positive journey, even with lots of snow.

Prior to this ministry assignment when I took new roles at other churches, I prepared only in these general ways: asking questions during the interview, searching the church's website, preparing for the physical move and new housing, and attending the perfunctory meet-and-greets. I gave little thought beforehand to what I needed to focus on during those first few months in my new job.

This time, however, before I took the position, I read three onboarding books written for the business leader that helped me create a framework for my onboarding plan. Along with *Every Pastor's First 180 Days*, I highly recommend *The First 90 Days, Updated and Expanded: Proven Strategies for Getting Up to Speed Faster and Smarter* by Michael D. Watkins. The author has created a nifty smartphone app, called *The First 90 Days*, that reinforces the book's content.

Each of the books I read had its particular strengths. I realized, however, that a pastor's world differs in many ways and some of the advice simply didn't apply to ministry. So I began to craft my own ministry onboarding plan from a pastor's perspective. During my six months, I tweaked, religiously followed, and chronicled my onboarding journey, which ultimately led me to write *Every Pastor's First 180 Days*.

In a previous book,[11] I wrote about how our brains like certainty and dislike uncertainty. When we face uncertainty, the fight-flight part of our brains (the amygdala) goes on high alert and incites the release of neurotransmitters into our brain and the stress hormone cortisol into

---

11   Charles Stone, *Brain-Savvy Leaders: The Science of Significant Ministry* (Nashville, Tennessee: Abingdon Press, 2015).

our bloodstream. When our body stays on high alert for long periods of time, a state called allostatic load, cortisol can actually damage our body and brain. Well, the initial circumstances in my new job gave many reasons for my body to release loads of extra cortisol. Here are some of them:

- First, I began my lead pastor role with two key positions unfilled. The month prior to my coming, the executive pastor left, and within two months our worship pastor left and another pastor was on his way out. Both were full-time roles. And the part-time senior adult pastor had also previously left.

- Second, not only would those staff holes put more on my busy plate, but we lacked the money to hire replacements. The first week I arrived, we were already in a budget hole by over $100,000. We had zero cash in the bank, which required the board to approve a line of credit just so we could pay our bills. We were well into spending from that line of credit, and I saw no way to fill those positions any time soon. At our continued rate of giving, I projected a $350,000 deficit by the end of our fiscal year.

- Third, the second week I was on staff, a huge snowstorm dumped three feet of snow on Saturday night, forcing us to cancel services, the first time that had happened in the church in over twenty years. If you live in a cold climate and have had to cancel services due to weather, you seldom make up the lost offering. Our financial picture looked even bleaker.

- Fourth, the week I arrived, the elder board fired and unfired a staff person because they had made a decision based on incomplete information. This created considerable angst among the current staff. So I began my first week with a spooked staff.

- Fifth, after two months and multiple information-gathering meetings, two significant problems surfaced. First, I realized we had our own worship wars as two camps had formed, one contemporary and the other traditional. Second, a huge void of trust in leadership existed, especially from the senior adults. Many of the seniors did not like what had happened in the past and distrusted leadership.
- Sixth, although I didn't notice it during my candidating process, I quickly realized a key demographic fact: over 55 percent of the church was over sixty-five, and the number of younger people was considerably smaller than I had assumed. We had a great group of seniors, but I knew that if we were to grow, we faced an uphill battle reaching a younger demographic.
- Seventh, very few ministry systems existed, such as ministry descriptions, volunteer training, or communication processes.
- And finally, on top of those surprises, I faced incredibly high expectations as the church voted by to call me with a 100 percent vote. (No pressure, eh?)

Even with those challenges, God used my onboarding plan to keep me focused, help me gain more certainty (resulting in less personal anxiety), and experience a very positive first six months. I believe an onboarding plan can do the same for you in your new role. In the next section, I explain the first concept, *Prioritize Self and Family Care*, which can help you begin your personal onboarding plan on a good footing.

Earlier I mentioned a smartphone app by the author of *The First 90 Days*. This quote from that app suggests a sound reason to onboard well so that you can lead at your best.

Ultimately, leadership is about leverage. You are just one person, after all. To be successful, you'll need to mobilize the energy of many others in your organization (church)… [my notation]. If you do the right things, your vision, expertise, and drive can serve as seed crystals in your new organization (church). If you don't, you can get caught in damaging cycles that are difficult—if not impossible—to escape from.

The onboarding plan this book helps you create can help you avoid those damaging cycles.

CHAPTER 1

PRIORITIZE SELF AND FAMILY CARE

It must be God first, God second, and God third.
— Oswald Chambers

⌐⌐

Chapter snapshot:

Prioritize self and family care
Avidly overcommunicate
Listen and learn
Manage change wisely

A healthy ministry flows out of a healthy body, a healthy soul, and a healthy family. For your first six months to go well, it's important to prioritize your mental and physical health and your family as well. In this chapter, you'll learn how to keep those healthy.

New Beginnings

Anytime a family moves, it's normal to experience some stress. As you might expect, the challenge of my new job added more stress. In our case, though, we faced some out-of-the-ordinary sources of stress. We entered not only into a new church culture but a new country culture as well. We had to learn how to be Canadian. The immigration process required that we jump through many hoops. The Canadian system of medical care differed from the U.S. system, and we had to navigate it. I needed to learn how things got done in my new Canadian church.

After three weeks of being in Canada, I excitedly began my first day in the office. I relished the new opportunity and began the ministry running at full throttle. During the first few weeks, I kept relatively good margins. However, our lack of staffing and the tight budget added to the general uncertainty that newness can cause. It began to take its toll. After a few weeks, I felt constantly exhausted. I wasn't sleeping well. It seemed that I was always *on.* A "hurried soul" mentality began to set in. And my family began to feel the brunt of my stress. So what I share in this chapter reflects what I learned about self and family care even though I didn't do a great job myself.

Research tells us that those in ministry face a higher incidence of anxiety, burnout, and depression than the average person in our churches. The younger and less experienced a minister and the more perfectionistic they tend to be, the greater the chances they will face these problems.[12] Remember, every new ministry will offer many opportunities to NOT take care of yourself or your family. Remind yourself that when you take care of yourself (your body and your soul), you will have the energy and motivation to take care of your family. Family care will translate into self-care since your family is your primary support group.

In the pages that follow, I discuss four distinct areas that impact our emotional, spiritual, and physical health and the health of our marriages and families. It behooves us to pay attention to each area. *Prioritize Self and Family Care* is crucial to sustaining long-lasting, healthy leadership; therefore, this chapter is the longest. Here are the four areas.

---

12   L. Harris, "Burnout and Depression on Clergy: A Research Paper | Eaglecrest Counseling Center," accessed November 2, 2015, http://eaglecrestcounseling. com/2010/07/burnout-and-depression-on-clergy-a-research-paper/.

- Pain/woundedness: process it.
- Expectations: clarify them.
- Stress: manage it.
- A safe friend: find one.

Process Your Pain and Woundedness

We all carry baggage not only from our family of origin but also from our previous ministry experiences. For some, that baggage may feel like a light daypack. For others, it may feel like a one-hundred-pound duffle bag. These factors influence how heavy your baggage feels.

- *Your overall emotional health.* If you come into your new setting already stressed, you won't have much internal reserve before you redline. You'll "spill over" more easily when jostled by ministry demands and conflict.
- *Your personality type influenced by your genetic makeup.* Some people are more genetically predisposed toward anxiety and depression than others. Our genetic makeup accounts for about 1/3 of our ability to be happy and enjoy life.[13] The remaining 2/3, however, gives us lots of leverage to change, manage stress, and bounce back from difficulties. It's called resilience.
- *Your previous ministry setting.* If you came from a difficult situation, you'll need to pay more attention to the suggestions in this chapter.

So before you hit the ground running, it's important to deal with your hurt, woundedness, and unresolved emotional pain as much as possible. If this seems self-serving, look to the words of Jesus Himself. In response to a Pharisee's question about the greatest commandment, Jesus said, "'Love the Lord your God with all your heart and with all your soul and with all

---

13   "Can Happiness Be Genetic?", Psychology Today, accessed November 20, 2015, http://www.psychologytoday.com/blog/media-spotlight/201302/can-happiness-be-genetic.

your mind.' This is the first and greatest commandment. And the second is like it: 'Love your neighbor as yourself'" (Matt 22:37-39 NIV). So Jesus' own words remind us we should love ourselves and be kind to ourselves, which encompasses processing our own hurts and pain. Research tells us that pastors who are kinder to themselves when they fail or don't meet others' expectations are less prone to burnout.[14]

I learned this insight several years ago when I transitioned to a church in California from a church in Atlanta. After we moved, I was surprised when I began to grieve. I recall one day as I assembled an outdoor tool shed how deep feelings of sadness suddenly swept over me. I wasn't sad about my new role as teaching pastor. The new possibilities excited me. However, my emotions reminded me that I must deal with my feelings of loss from leaving the church that my wife and I had planted fourteen years earlier.

In a later ministry setting in Chicago, I faced significant conflict with two leaders that left deep wounds. During the year and a half between that church and my new church in Canada, I had to process this new pain I had carried with me from that church. I share later in the chapter what I did to help me release my hurt.

How to Deal with Your Pain

Although I don't write in depth about how to deal with pain in this book, I suggest a few ideas below that might help:

First, admit that some leftover baggage from your prior ministry may still be weighing you down. These questions may help bring to the surface unresolved issues that could potentially derail your new start.

1. With whom did you experience the greatest conflict or the greatest hurt?

2. How did you deal with those conflicts? Passively, aggressively, biblically?

---

14   Laura K. Barnard and John F. Curry, "The Relationship of Clergy Burnout to Self-Compassion and Other Personality Dimensions," *Pastoral Psychology* 61, no. 2 (May 21, 2011): 149–63, https:// DOI 10.1007/s11089-011-0377-0

3. When you think of that person(s), do you feel significant anger, rage, or bitterness rise to your awareness? Or are the emotions more akin to mild disappointment or sadness?
4. Do you feel that any of those conflictual relationships lie unresolved and that resolution remains possible? Or do you feel that you did what you could to resolve the issues?
5. How would you rate where you stand in relation to this person(s)/ issue(s): distraught, hurting but managing, coping OK, or in good shape with occasional twinges of loss or pain?
6. Is God prompting you to do anything to resolve this pain?

Second, take specific steps to deal with the emotional baggage. When my pain was most acute prior to my coming to Canada, I sought professional help. I consulted a counselor for several sessions, and I hired a coach who helped me process my woundedness. An objective third party can help you see issues to which you may be blind. I recommend that every ministry leader find a good friend, and I discuss this in more detail later in this chapter.

As you process your pain, God may want you to initiate an act of kindness toward the person(s) who may have hurt you in your prior ministry. During my consulting/writing days prior to my move to Canada, our family joined a local church near the small lake house we had moved into. I immediately bonded with the pastor and volunteered to serve. Each Sunday, I learned something new from his solid preaching. One day his sermon dealt with turning the other cheek and loving your enemies despite the pain they may have caused you. Like a lightning bolt, I felt God impress me to send a restaurant gift card to both leaders who had hurt me the most at my prior church. I included a nice note with each card. After I took that simple obedient step, God began to close that painful chapter in my life, although I still feel an occasional tinge of emotion when I recall those experiences.

God used my pain to teach me, and He can use your pain to teach you as well. However, we must never allow pain to fester in our souls. I encourage you to inventory your previous ministry experience and bring out into the open any stuffed or hidden pain. If you don't deal with it now, it will leak out, insidiously drain you, and quite possibly derail you before you gain traction in your new role.

Establish and Clarify Realistic Expectations

The word "expectation" comes from the Latin word *expectationem*, meaning "an awaiting." When you begin a new ministry role, lots of people are awaiting your performance, forecasting your behavior, and making assumptions about what you will or won't do in the future. Often such expectations conflict with each another. What you expect may not align with what your boss or board expects. Your staff and volunteers' expectation may differ from yours. Your family's wishes may conflict with yours. And your aspirations may even differ from God's plan for your new role.

In this section, I deal only with setting and clarifying expectations you have of yourself and those of your family. In a later chapter, we'll look at how to clarify expectations with your boss or board. Consider these four realistic expectations.

Expectation 1: *I will choose to be ok even if everybody doesn't like me.*

This one will probably challenge you, as I learned from the research for my third book, *People-Pleasing Pastors: Avoiding the Pitfalls of Approval Motivated Leadership.* I discovered that anywhere from 79 percent to 90 percent of pastors admitted that people pleasing affected their leadership on some level. Even though my first year at WestPark went quite well, I didn't please everybody.

In WestPark's tradition, although the elder board makes the recommendation for the new lead pastor, the church has the final say. In other words, they voted whether to hire me. I had hoped for at least a 90 percent approval even though the constitution didn't require that high a threshold. I remember the night they voted. We had driven back to our hotel room and received the call from the board chair. He was on his cell's speaker phone so that those at the meeting could hear our conversation.

He said, "Charles, the vote has come in. What do you think the vote was?" I replied, "Well, I hope it's a *Yes*. And I assume there are some *No's* as well." His reply? "Charles, you got a 100 percent vote." I was floored, excited, and worried at the same time. It felt good to get the affirmation. But at the same time, I felt significant pressure. The vote indicated they held high expectations for me. I wondered if I would be able to meet them.

During the first year, I wish I could say that no one left the church and everyone was happy. Most stayed, a few drifted away, and I received a few harsh emails and blunt comments. So I had to set my expectations that even if I led at the highest level I could, some people would not respond, would not like me or the direction I was taking the church, and eventually leave.

Expectation 2: *I will clarify, negotiate, and respect my family's agreed-upon expectations for me.*

Whether or not you verbalize the expectations your family has for you in your new role, they exist. Acknowledge that you can't avoid the disruption and frustration your family will feel from the move, so bring these issues out into the open. Talk about them. Ask your spouse and kids what they expect from you in the first six months. Just listen to them, even though you may disagree with them, and come to a mutual understanding of their and your expectations.

During the first few months, the church will demand more of your time than normal. Your schedule may seem out of balance for a while. Don't be surprised. You will probably attend more meetings and events early on as you get to know the people in your new church. Expect this and talk about it with your family. Negotiate what you all feel is a reasonable schedule in the first few months, given the intensity of a new ministry.

And remember that your family, if you are married, will probably adjust to your new setting slower than you will. Your new role offers the excitement of a new job, staff and/or volunteers you'll spend time with, and a more regular routine than your spouse will enjoy. In many ways, your spouse will face more uncertainty than you will. Unless he or she takes an immediate job, they must create new routines, get the kids situated, learn where to shop, find the family doctor, and face multiple other changes.

Finding new friendships probably won't come as easily for a woman as for you (if you're a guy) since your new role includes built-in relationships like staff, volunteers, and boards. You, and especially your family, will face uncertainty, and the body can suffer from the stress uncertainty brings. As Michael Watkins wrote, "The stresses of your professional transition can amplify the strain of your family's transition."[15]

As I wrote earlier, it's important to remember that our brain craves certainty and predictability. It wants to know what's next. Certainty feels rewarding because it gives the brain a nice boost of the feel-good neurotransmitter, dopamine. However, when our brain deals with ongoing uncertainty and ambiguity, it affects us and our loved ones in negative ways. Provide your family more certainty by letting them know your schedule and routines, even though things are more hectic. Try to begin your family rituals and routines as quickly as you can, and preserve them. Block regular family time into your schedule. Just as you schedule appointments with church people, do the same for your family so that busyness doesn't crowd them out.

When you face a particularly demanding week, let your family know ahead of time and schedule more family time the following week. Don't let your family suffer, but try to help them understand that the first six months will demand more of you than normal.

After the first six months, however, reestablish a new normalcy. Invite key people to hold you accountable to bring your routine back to a healthy balance after that time. Remember that you will enjoy the adrenaline rush the new role offers while your family will have to deal with your mental distraction and absence. Don't forget that they must also deal with their own stress that the move will bring.

Expectation 3: *I will take care of my body and my soul.*

Because a new ministry role inevitably involves a greater demand on your time, you'll be tempted to let those demands crowd out body and soul care. Skipping your morning run or your devotional time or grabbing

---

15   Watkins, *The First 90 Days,* p 232.

a donut at the coffee shop may be the easiest thing to do with a crammed scheduled. Sometimes it is the only choice. But when those choices become habits, not only will your physical and spiritual health suffer, but your leadership will as well. You must maintain the physical and spiritual stamina to lead well, especially in the beginning.

In my first six months, I scheduled devotional time and exercise into my Outlook calendar five to six times a week. I didn't always keep those personal appointments, but for the most part, I did. I'm convinced those habits contributed to a strong first six months. Exercise, healthy eating, soul care, and weekly days off all help combat the negative effects of chronic stress, which I discuss in more detail below. Since the first six months seem more like a sprint, we must pay extra attention to body and soul care during that time.

I recommend my most recent book, *Holy Noticing: The Bible, Your Brain, and the Mindful Space Between Moments.* It's a toolbox on how to learn to live in the present moment without trying to get to a better one. It's a spiritual discipline, often called mindfulness in today's vernacular, that has transformed my life and can transform yours as well. Although in this current book I don't devote a lot of space to spiritual health, I am not minimizing its importance. You'll find many good books on soul care that can guide you. Please don't neglect your soul, for out of a healthy soul flows healthy ministry.

Scripture often reinforces the value of body and soul care. King David reminds us to take care of our souls in Psalms 62:5: *Find rest, O my soul, in God alone.* And the Apostle Paul reminds us in 1 Corinthians 6 that because our bodies are temples of the Holy Spirit, we should take care of them.

Stress: manage it.

Stress is unavoidable in a new ministry role, and up to a point, it actually helps motivate us. But prolonged, chronic stress diminishes performance (it's called the Yerkes-Dodson law[16]) and hurts our bodies

---

16   "Yerkes - Dodson Law," *Psychestudy* (blog), November 17, 2017, https://www.psychestudy.com/general/motivation-emotion/yerkes-dodson-law.

and brains. Moving is one of the highest stress-causing life events. One interesting study found that a move can make us look and feel two years older.[17] And if you add that to normal ministry stress, your health, your family, and your ministry will suffer if you don't manage it early on. Pete Scazzero describes what unmanaged stress can do:

> *Most of us are overscheduled and preoccupied; we are starved for time, exhausted from the endless needs around us. Who has time to enjoy Jesus, our spouses, our children, life itself?*
>
> *We assume we'll catch up on our sleep some other time. The space we need for replenishing our soul and relaxing can happen later. Few of us have time for fun and hobbies. We don't have a life! There is simply too much work to be done for God.*[18]

Stress is very real in ministry, as reflected in the LifeWay Research study in 2015 to which I referred in the introductory chapter. How do you know that you are overly stressed? First, you can download and take a helpful Ministry Burnout Inventory∞ at www.charlesstone.com/freebies. Or you can evaluate yourself right now by asking which of these statements are true for you. If two or more of these statements are true, you're probably not managing stress very well:

1. You quickly walk by someone at church or at the office to avoid a conversation simply because you don't have the energy to engage.
2. Fun in ministry and life seems to have disappeared.
3. When you come home your spouse often says, "You look terrible."
4. When you come home, you feel like immediately going to bed.

---

17   Kyrsty Hazell, "Can Moving House Cause Premature Ageing?," The Huffington Post UK, July 11, 2011, http://www.huffingtonpost.co.uk/2011/11/07/stress-of-buying-a-house-ages-us-by-two-years_n_1079444.html.

18   Pete Scazzero, "Skimming," Leadership Journal, accessed May 20, 2019, https://www.christianitytoday.com/pastors/2009/winter/skimming.html.

5. You can't shake free the anxiety that seems to cling to your soul.
6. Small things that once didn't bother you now set you off.
7. You often ruminate over and rehearse negative issues in your ministry and/or life.
8. You easily default to worst-case scenario thinking.
9. You feel anger coursing deep within.
10. You're not sleeping well.

So what can you do to better manage stress? First, as you begin your new role, keep in mind these insights about stress:

1. Allostatic load

This term describes the wear and tear on our body resulting from chronic stress.[19] Our bodies have limits, and when under stress for long periods of time, they suffer. Prolonged stress causes sustained high levels of the stress hormone cortisol, which, along with an overabundance of other neurotransmitters and hormones, can cause heart problems, weight gain, impaired immunity, decreased memory due to brain cell atrophy, and diminished brain functioning.[20]

2. Power stress

Richard Boyatzis and Annie McKee, authors of *Resonant Leadership,* coined this phrase to describe a kind of stress unique to leaders. "Power stress is part of the experience that results from the exercise of influence and sense of responsibility felt in leadership positions."[21] McKee and Boyatzis

---

19 Charles Stone, *Brain-Savvy Leaders: The Science of Significant Ministry* (Abingdon Press, 2015), Kindle e-book loc 1557.

20 "How Stress Affects Your Brain - Madhumita Murgia," TED-Ed, accessed August 19, 2016, https://ed.ted.com/lessons/how-stress-affects-your-brain-madhumita-murgia.

21 Richard E. Boyatzis and Annie McKee, *Resonant Leadership: Renewing Yourself and Connecting with Others Through Mindfulness, Hope, and Compassion,* 1 edition (Boston: Harvard Business Review Press, 2005), Kindle e-book loc 3479.

explain that when the demands of leadership get so high and leaders fail to manage it, they risk becoming trapped in what they call the *Sacrifice Syndrome*. Sometimes we leaders feel so overly responsible for the success of our ministries or churches that we get caught in a vicious cycle of unhealthy sacrifice for others that leads to burnout.

3. Continuous partial attention

Linda Stone, author and consultant, developed this phrase[22] to describe the mental trap we easily fall into when we constantly scan our surroundings to look for the best opportunities to spend our time on. It happens when we skim and pay attention only partially. When this happens to leaders, they will fail to focus on the most important tasks at hand and get further behind on mission-critical issues. Then they must rush to get the important things done, which further contributes to chronic stress.

4. Multitasking

Multitasking is a myth. Author David Rock notes, "Many leaders have convinced themselves that multitasking leads to greater productivity. However, researchers have shown that when we try to process two mental tasks at once, our mental capacity can drop from that of a Harvard MBA to that of an eight-year-old. And it can reduce our mental capacities as if we missed a night's sleep or smoked pot."[23] Multitasking can even diminish our long-term memory.[24] It can add up to a 40 percent loss of productivity in

---

22 "Linda Stone," in *Wikipedia, the Free Encyclopedia*, July 6, 2015, https://en.wikipedia. org/w/index.php?title=Linda_Stone&oldid=670142710.

23 David Rock, *Your Brain at Work: Strategies for Overcoming Distraction, Regaining Focus, and Working Smarter All Day Long*, 1st Ed. edition (New York: HarperBusiness, 2009), Kindle e-book loc 682.

24 Karin Foerde, Barbara J. Knowlton, and Russell A. Poldrack, "Modulation of Competing Memory Systems by Distraction," *Proceedings of the National Academy of Sciences* 103, no. 31 (August 1, 2006): 11778–83, https://doi.org/10.1073/ pnas.0602659103.

a day.[25] With busy schedules the first six months, such loss of productivity will only exacerbate your stress.

Consider these specific practices that can lessen your stress:

1. Exercise.

For decades, we've known how exercise benefits our body. But recent research[26] has discovered that it benefits our brains and reduces stress as well. When we exercise, it causes our brains to release a protein called brain-derived neurotrophic factor (BDNF), which has been dubbed Miracle-Gro for the brain. It encourages new neuronal growth and protects brain cells from the effects of stress.

2. Statio.

Statio[27] is a Christian monastic practice that we might call a *mini-transition* between events of the day. It's those in-between moments when we pause before going from one task to the next. It allows us to break our hurry, obtain closure from the prior task, and prepare our hearts and minds for what comes next. Leaders who practice this can turn down their body's fight-flight system (the sympathetic nervous system) and engage the rest and digest system (the parasympathetic system), which makes us calmer and reduces the impact of stress.

3. Sleep.

In my previous book I noted the value of sleep: "When we don't get enough sleep, we rob our brains of important neural functions because the

---

25   Ron Friedman, "The Cost of Continuously Checking Email," Harvard Business Review, accessed May 20,2019, https://hbr.org/2014/07/the-cost-of-continuously-checking-email.

26   John J. Ratey and Eric Hagerman, *Spark: The Revolutionary New Science of Exercise and the Brain*, Reprint edition (Little, Brown, and Company, 2013).

27   Daniel Schroeder, "Statio - The Pause That Refreshes," EzineArticles, accessed May 20, 2019, http://ezinearticles.com/?Statio---The-Pause-That-Refreshes&id=3734606.

brain is actually very active during sleep. Although the brain never really shuts down, it's only truly at rest during non-REM sleep, which accounts for only 20 percent of our normal sleep cycle. During the other 80 percent, sleep helps the brain encode, strengthen, stabilize, and consolidate our memories from the day. Our brain replays what we have learned during the day to make our memories stick. Sleep also plays an important role in learning."[28] So sleep is another effective way to combat stress.

4. Get off the grid.

In our 24-7 connected world, our smartphones can actually keep us on high alert and in stress mode. I find that if I choose a twenty-four-hour period (my Sabbath, which is usually Saturday) when I don't respond to or seldom check email, I'm much more at peace. Getting off the grid helps disengage my mind and slow my internal pace. Turning *off* the automatic notifications function on my smartphone and my computer has also helped me get off the grid.

A Safe Friend: Find One

God made us for relationship with one other. We were made for community, and we all want good friends. A good friend who can serve as a safe sounding board is essential in a new ministry role. But what do good friends look like? What do they do or not do? In Philippians, the most intimate of the thirteen letters the Apostle Paul wrote that help form the New Testament, we see a portrait of what to look for in a friend. In Philippians 1:3-11, Paul provides a template. Consider these five behaviors to look for and ask God to provide you one (or more) in your new role. A good friend will act in the following ways:

1. A good friend will remember the best about you (v. 3).

When Paul prayed for his friends in the church in the city of Philippi, his thoughts of them brought him great joy. He chose to focus on their good

---

28 Stone, *Brain-Savvy Leaders*, Kindle e-book loc 1665.

qualities rather than on their limitations and weaknesses. He remembered their best.

2. A good friend will give his or her best to you (v. 5, 7).

Paul wrote that he *had them in his heart.* He fully gave himself to them by giving them the deepest part of himself, his heart. When he described their strong, intimate relationship, He used the word *koinonia,* which means deep partnership. Paul was not a relationship skimmer. Rather, he gave himself fully to these special friends.

3. A good friend will encourage the best in you (v. 6).

He was confident that God would finish the work that He had begun in them. He emphasized that truth and sought to bring out their best. Good friends will bring out your best. Author Liz Wiseman, who studied 150 leaders for her book, *Multipliers: How the Best Leaders Make Everyone Smarter,* discovered that there are two kinds of leaders: multipliers and diminishers. Multipliers bring out the best in others by amplifying their strengths, encouraging them, and empowering them. Diminishers do the opposite. They drain others by having all the answers, micro-managing, and being self-focused. Good friends will always seek to be multipliers in your life.

4. A good friend will pray the best for you (v. 9).

Paul fervently prayed for his friends. He prayed that they would love Jesus and others more, learn more about God, and live out the truths of God's Word in their conduct and character. Good friends will pray that those three qualities will become a reality in their friends.

5. A good friend will expect the best from you (vs. 10-11).

Good friends will hold you accountable. They will tell you what you may not want to hear because they will expect the best from you. They won't let you settle for what is just good. They will challenge you to do and be your best.

When you enter your new role, pray that God will provide you a good, safe friend who embodies these qualities. I strongly encourage you to find a friend of the same gender as you. He or she could be in your church, a leader at another church, or even a coach with whom you enter a professional relationship. I've had safe friends in all three categories.

A good friend during your first six months and beyond can help you onboard well. They can give you perspective when you've lost yours. They can ask questions to make you think deeply about the challenges in your new role rather than just giving you advice. They can help you see your blind spots and can affirm you when you most need it. I've provided a download called the *Safe Friend Checklist*,∞ which gives you an extensive checklist to help you find a safe friend.

In this chapter, we've unpacked the first pillar of the onboarding acronym PALM, "P" for *Prioritize Self and Family Care*. In the next chapter, we'll look at the next two, *Avidly Over Communicate* and *Listen and Learn,* as they represent the proverbial two sides of the same coin.

———

Pause and reflect question: On a scale of 1–10, how would those closest to you rate how well you're living out, *Prioritize Self and Family Care?*

Next-step application: Look again at the four areas related to *Prioritize Self and Family Care* below. Pick one the one you feel needs the most attention. Write down one practical step you could take within the next twenty-four hours to develop that area. Share it with your spouse and then do it.

- Pain/woundedness: process it.
- Expectations: clarify them.
- Stress: manage it.
- A sounding board: find one.

CHAPTER 2

AVIDLY OVERCOMMUNICATE
AND LISTEN AND LEARN

There's a lot of difference between listening and hearing.
— G.K. Chesterton

The ear of the leader must ring with the voices of the people.
— Woodrow Wilson

❧

Chapter snapshot:

Prioritize self and family care
Avidly overcommunicate
Listen and learn
Manage change wisely

Just as a coin has two sides, so does information flow. In your new role, you will *share* information through various communication channels and *take in* information by listening and learning. Effective communication requires that you answer five critical questions to maximize your message and build credibility.

1. Who needs to know?
2. Why do they need to know?
3. What do they need to know?
4. When do they need to know it?
5. How can I help them know it?

Good listening requires that you assume these four essential listening postures so you learn what you need to know.
1. A rookie mindset
2. Self-awareness
3. Engaged presence
4. An action bias

Part 1: Avidly Overcommunicate

I wrote earlier that when I arrived in Canada, I hit the ground running. However, rather than hitting the ground running, I suggest that you instead hit the ground listening because you don't know as much as you think you may know. When I referred to *hit the ground running*, I meant that I was busy meeting people and attending meetings, running from one meeting and task to the next. However, during those early months, fortunately, I did less *telling* than listening. I mostly listened and kept people in the know about what I was learning by overcommunicating to the church. And although *Every Pastor's First 180 Days* targets the first six months, I encourage you to apply these concepts for the duration of your ministry leadership.

As I've written, the brain craves certainty and dislikes uncertainty. Uncertainty activates the brain's fear circuits, and when that happens, we tend to make up stories in our minds that probably aren't true. It's called the negativity bias. We have five times more negative circuits in our brain that look for what's wrong than we have positive circuits that look for what is right.[29] We are biologically biased to assume the worst, and

---

29   Roy F. Baumeister et al., "Bad Is Stronger than Good," *Review of General Psychology* 5, no. 4 (2001): 323–70, https://doi.org/10.1037/1089-2680.5.4.323.

people naturally make negative assumptions when left in an information vacuum. This heightens our need for clear, concise, positive, and timely communication.

The Apostle Paul speaks to our negativity bias when he writes these words to help us counter that bias: *Finally, brothers, whatever is true, whatever is noble, whatever is right, whatever is pure, whatever is lovely, whatever is admirable — if anything is excellent or praiseworthy — think about such things* (Phil 4:8 NIV).

I've combined two of the PALM concepts in this chapter because you can't do one effectively without doing the other effectively. Listening feeds the "giving out" side of communication, and vice versa. Thomas Neff and James Citrin, authors of *You're in Charge, Now What?* write, "Communicating is much more than promulgating a message. It is just as much the gathering of disparate thoughts and information that will help shape the message."[30] So it's essential to develop a communication plan that includes giving out and taking in important information. These five essential questions can guide your communication plan in the first six months.

1. Who needs to know?
2. Why do they need to know?
3. What do they need to know?
4. When do they need to know?
5. How can I help them know it?

Who needs to know?

As you begin your new role, clarify the people and groups who will need to know what you're doing and what you plan to do. Who they are will determine what you communicate, the sequence in which you communicate, and the frequency. And keep in mind concentric circles of communication. Key leaders and stakeholders should be the first to receive communication before larger groups and the church receive it. When you do that, you honor your leaders.

---

30 Thomas J. Neff and James M. Citrin, *You're in Charge, Now What?: The 8 Point Plan,* Reprint edition (New York: Crown Business, 2007), Kindle e-book loc 3356.

As the lead pastor in my situation, I needed to communicate with four distinct groups: the church as a whole, my staff, the elder board, and the broader group of volunteers. If you are a worship leader, your group might include the lead pastor, your worship team, and your tech team. If you are a student pastor, your group might be your supervisor, your youth leaders, the students, and parents. Once you've determined those groups, you should ask the next four questions about each group.

Why do they need to know?

The church needed to know that I was not going to come in and blow up the place by making radical changes. They needed to know that I really was listening and learning. Our staff needed to begin building trust in me, and I needed to build their confidence. Healthy communication helps do that. Later, I devote an entire chapter, chapter 9, to building trust. Our elders needed to know that I was a team player and would not run roughshod over their authority and ideas.

What do they need to know?

Not every group needs to receive the exact same information. You'll need to carefully determine what kind of information goes to one group and what kind goes to another. Don't get hung up here or complicate matters on this point. Just keep in mind that although some information will overlap, some groups will naturally need more or less information than other groups. Tailor what you communicate depending on the specific group's need to know.

For example, in the first few months, I provided a weekly report to the elder board that detailed my activity. I summarized that report in a paragraph that I included in the weekly church bulletin called, "Where's Waldo...aka, What's Charles been up to this week." The people loved that quick summary, as I usually included something interesting about our family life (with permission from them of course). This helped them feel like they knew me better as a person. Here's my first *Where's Waldo.*

Humbled by the Remembrance Day service I attended [this is the equivalent to Memorial Day for readers in the U.S.]. First official elder's meeting (great group of leaders). Over a dozen meetings with most of the staff (an honor to work with these servants). Loving my study on Nehemiah (we begin the series this coming week-invite a friend). Jazzed to be here!

When do they need to know it?

This question reinforces the need to be timely with your communication. The more timely you communicate, the better. Last minute, hasty communication is seldom effective. Whatever pattern of communication you develop, stay consistent. If my reports to the elders had been hit and miss, I wouldn't have been able to build rapport and trust with them as fast as I did.

In a crisis, communicate as quickly as possible. In one instance, a high-profile volunteer with influence over a particular group abruptly quit and left the church. We immediately sent that group an email and called a meeting. We appropriately explained the situation, apologized for our part in the disagreement, and fielded questions. This quick communication put out a smoldering fire that could have blazed out of control. In a crisis, get ahead of the grapevine or at least parallel to it.

In another example, the Saturday before our second Sunday at WestPark, a blizzard dumped three feet of snow on the city and we had to cancel services. We were already deep into a financial hole and missing a Sunday only made things worse. On the following Monday, we sent a letter to the church explaining our finances and included a copy of the bulletin we had printed for the Sunday we had canceled. God blessed our offering the next Sunday, and we almost made it up the following week. A senior adult even remarked how well that gesture communicated to the church.

How can I help them know it?

This question relates to the various mediums available to you for communication. You'll want to maximize your mediums depending on your church's culture. As an example, I've listed below how I communicated to each group. You can download the Church Communication Template,∞ a tool that can help you organize your communication plan.

- Our elder board
    - I shared a verbal update report at our bimonthly meetings.
    - I created a weekly email update that explained what I had done that week.
    - I emailed them our weekly staff agenda/report so they'd know what the staff was doing.
    - I create a sixty-day progress report.
    - I created a ninety-day action plan.

- The church
    - I placed a *Where's Waldo* blurb in each week's bulletin.
    - We created a weekly e-news that we sent to the entire church. The e-news included upcoming events and praises of what God was doing.
    - I sent the church via email and snail mail a ninety-day update and a six-month update. You can download an example of my Ninety-Day Progress Report I sent to the church.∞
    - I preached on Nehemiah the first six months, which naturally allowed me to deal with issues such as unity, criticism, and vision.
    - When I preached, I often included snippets on what I was learning the first six months as a newcomer to the church and to Canada.
    - We began to use social media more effectively.

- Staff
    - I let the staff know via email if my schedule significantly changed (i.e., if I was going to be late coming into the office).

- I created staff meeting agendas and invited them to help build those agendas. I've included a Staff Meeting Agenda Template you can download.∞
- I created a weekly staff update where each staff person answered four questions (more on this in chapter 6). We then shared this report with the entire staff and elders.
- We started a worship planning meeting to involve other key worship team members to help plan and evaluate our services.

- Volunteers
  - I interviewed several dozen people one-on-one and held a collaborative fact-finding process called an appreciative inquiry (more about appreciative inquiry in chapter 6).
  - We started a quarterly leadership community meeting for all volunteers. At that meeting, we'd cast vision, build community, and share important information before the church as a whole heard about it.

So you can see how I tailored what and when I sent information to various groups and people. As you craft your communication plan, keep these other communication concepts in mind as well.

1. Communication is both formal (i.e., emails) and informal (i.e., body language and tone). Be as intentional with your informal communication as you are with your formal communication. People are watching you. What you do and say will be magnified. Don't become paranoid, but stay aware.
2. Respect concentric circles of impact. Some key individuals and groups should receive communication before others do. In my case, elders hear first, then staff, then the church. Also, when you share information with specific groups before the church as a whole hears, you make them insiders, which fosters goodwill (more about that in the next chapter).

3. Practice good email etiquette. Make sure your emails communicate a positive tone. It's easy for others to assume something negative if you don't carefully craft your emails. Remember the negativity bias.

4. Tell stories. Stories move people's hearts and stick in their minds longer than facts and figures. For example, at the end of several updates, I included a story that illustrated God at work in our church. As we prepared for our offering each week, we showed a picture of a ministry on-screen made possible through the church's offerings. This helped translate dollars and cents to something tangible by putting a face on people's giving.

5. Maximize social media. It's ubiquitous in our culture today. Pick one or two mediums and initially focus your efforts there. Become proficient in the medium the people in your church use most often.

6. Don't fixate on trying to make your communication plan perfect. Be careful about spending too much time on it. Keep other important activities at the forefront as well.

7. Keep in mind this key truth. "How well you communicate is determined not by how well you say things but by how well you are understood."[31] Occasionally ask people in your church how effective they perceive your communication. Adjust your plan based on what you learn.

Part 2: Listen and Learn

We've probably all told ourselves at some point in our leadership, "If only I had known (blank)." It relates to the saying, *We don't know what we don't know.* When we make decisions based on faulty assumptions, things seldom go well. For example, in my church in Chicago when we received our offering, we used cloth offering bags with a handle because it afforded people greater privacy. At WestPark, we used traditional offering plates.

---

31   Ibid, Kindle e-book loc 3505.

One day I decided that we'd dispense with the plates and buy offering bags until our long-term admin staffer suggested we not do that. She informed me that a church member had hand-made the plates from a tree that used to sit on the church property. I changed my mind and she helped spare me from a potential stumble. I didn't know what I didn't know.

Neff and Citrin reinforce these ideas with these words. "There's this adrenaline rush for new leaders that you might as well just let work its way out. But even during the adrenaline rush, the most important thing is to listen. Listen and listen and listen. Process the information you receive and integrate it with your own prior understanding and then cycle it. The process itself breeds commitment."[32] And Susan Cain, author of the best-selling book, *Quiet*, noted, "We have two ears and one mouth, and we should use them proportionally."[33]

Listening is one of the most powerful tools in your onboarding toolbox. Why is it so important? Because when others feel truly listened to, it physically feels good. When we disclose something about ourselves to another, it triggers the same good sensation in our brains that we get from eating or from receiving money.[34] Good listening impacts people at a deep level.

As you come into a new setting, you come with knowledge gaps. The sooner you fill in those knowledge gaps, the more effective you'll make your onboarding. I devote chapter 6 to the concept, *Define Reality*, where we'll delve more into the particulars of filling in these knowledge gaps. But in the remainder of this chapter, we'll examine some basic listening postures that can accelerate your learning. Michael Watkins notes, "It is essential to figure

---

32   Ibid, Kindle e-book loc 1073.

33   Susan Cain, *Quiet: The Power of Introverts in a World That Can't Stop Talking* (New York: Broadway Books, 2013), p 239.

34   Diana I. Tamir and Jason P. Mitchell, "Disclosing Information about the Self Is Intrinsically Rewarding," *Proceedings of the National Academy of Sciences* 109, no. 21 (May 22, 2012): 8038–43, erupt.

out what you need to know about your new organization and then to learn it as rapidly as you can. The more efficiently and effectively you learn, the more quickly you will close your window of vulnerability. You can identify potential problems that might erupt and take you off track."[35]

I suggest assuming these four listening postures that can help you find out what you need to know.

1. A rookie mindset
2. Self-awareness
3. Engaged presence
4. An action bias

A Rookie Mindset

A *rookie mindset* means that you come into your new role with an inquisitive perspective, not as a know-it-all. Liz Wiseman, author of *Rookie Smarts*, defines this mindset as, "how we think and act when we are mindful that we are doing something for the first time."[36] So be careful that you don't convey you have all the answers, because you don't (more about that in chapter 5, *Avoid Common Pitfalls*). Just because you've experienced success in prior ministries doesn't mean you should bring those same solutions to your new ministry setting. Avoid *imposing* your plan and ideas on others. Stay in a learning mode and remain teachable.

Max DePree, leadership author and former president of the Herman Miller furniture company, said that every leader will experience "temporary incompetence."[37] It's the awkward feeling we get when we just don't know what to do in a new leadership setting. If anyone was in a position to *not* experience this, he was. He took over the company's presidency from his brother, who took over from his father. He wrote about temporary incompetence as he took the reins of leadership even though he had been

35   Watkins, *The First 90 Days*, p. 46.

36   Liz Wiseman, *Rookie Smarts: Why Learning Beats Knowing in the New Game of Work*, (New York, HarperBusiness, 2014), p. 44

37   Scott Cormode, "Temporary Incompetence," n.d., accessed May 20, 2019, https://www.fuller.edu/next-faithful-step/classes/cf565/temporary-incompetence/.

literally raised in the company. He knew the company and the people in it. However, he didn't rely solely on his previous experience and knowledge to lead. He came in with a rookie mindset.

It's also important not to approach your listening and learning haphazardly. Rather, be intentional. I suggest that you create a set of common questions to provide a framework for your conversations. Answers from various people to these common questions can help patterns surface that you want to discover. They will also steer you to develop new questions to dig deeper into some patterns you see. In chapter 6, we'll look at some key questions to guide your listening and learning.

Self-Awareness

Self-awareness relates to being aware of the unhealthy listening practices we most easily default to. It's easy to slip into bad listening habits, and we must first become aware of them before we can change them. Lisa J. Downs, author and listening expert, and former president of the American Society for Training and Development, suggests that these are our worst listening habits.[38]

1. *Daydreaming:* thinking about unrelated topics when someone else is speaking.
2. *Debating:* carrying on an inner argument about what is being said.
3. *Judging:* letting negative views influence us.
4. *Problem-solving:* yearning to give unasked-for advice.
5. *Pseudo-listening:* pretending to be a good listener.
6. *Rehearsing:* planning what you want to say next. Stephen Covey has been often quoted as saying, "Most people do not listen with the intent to understand; they listen with the intent to reply."
7. *Stage hogging:* redirecting the conversation to suit your own goals.
8. *Ambushing:* gathering information to use against the other person.
9. *Selective listening:* only responding to the parts of the conversation that interest us.

---

38   Lisa J. Downs, *Listening Skills Training*, 1st edition (Alexandria, VA: ASTD, 2008).

10. *Defensive listening*: taking everything personally.
11. *Avoidant listening*: blocking out what you don't want to hear

If you mentally checked one or more of these bad habits, apply the following tips to become a better listener.

- Ask a close friend to give you feedback on how well they perceive that you listen.
- As you listen to someone, monitor your thoughts to catch yourself before you slip into one of the above habits. The term for monitoring your thoughts is called metacognition, thinking about your thinking.
- Talk less. The acronym **WAIT** has helped me listen better and talk less. It stands for **W**hy **A**m **I** **T**alking?

Engaged Presence

The only way to know your new ministry well is to listen, and listen a lot, especially in the early days. But listening is not simply hearing words from someone. Great listeners fully engage with those to whom they listen. When someone senses that you are truly present with them as you interact, you will gain credibility with them and learn important insights about your new setting.

Neuroscientist Andrew Newberg suggests in his book, *Words Can Change Your Brain*,[39] several science-based ways that help us maintain an engaged presence. I've summarized several here.

1. **When you listen, convey a relaxed demeanor.**
   Good listeners are not tense or frazzled. People pick up on our emotional tone, whether it's good or bad. It's called emotional contagion. When we're relaxed, it encourages the other person to relax as well.

---

39   Andrew Newberg and Mark Robert Waldman, *Words Can Change Your Brain: 12 Conversation Strategies to Build Trust, Resolve Conflict, and Increase Intimacy*, Reprint edition (New York: Plume, 2013).

2. **Stay fully present for the person you're talking to.**
    Good listeners aren't in a rush to move on to something or someone else. They don't look over the other person's shoulder. Rather, they make genuine eye contact. Eye contact stimulates the social networks of our brains, decreases the stress hormone cortisol, and increases the neurotransmitter oxytocin, which has been called the trust chemical, all of which enhance communication.

3. **Practice inner stillness and quietness.**
    This reflects the Psalmist's words in Psalm 46:10: *Be still and know that I am God (NIV)*. When we quiet our souls, we can pick up on nuanced messages others give us through facial expressions and body language. Words seldom fully convey what a person is thinking and feeling.

4. **Express appreciation and gratitude.**
    People yearn to hear encouragement from others, especially from their leaders. Newberg discovered that when we give a compliment at the end of a conversation, it's received better than one given at the beginning of a conversation.

5. **Speak with a warm tone.**
    A warm tone can set the stage for effective communication, whereas a harsh or negative tone can set up resistance in the other person. The writer of Proverbs reminds us of this with this counsel: *A gentle answer deflects anger, but harsh words make tempers flare* (Prov 15:1 NLT).

6. **Speak slowly.**
    When we speak slowly, those listening can comprehend us better and it can even help calm an anxious person.

7. **Speak briefly.**

Good listeners don't hog conversations with their words. Since our brains can only hold so much information at once in our working memory, speaking for shorter lengths of time improves communication by helping the listener retain more of what we say.

8. **Listen deeply.**

When we listen deeply, we don't let our minds wander. Rather, we give the other person the gift of our full attention and bodily presence.

An Action Bias

Action bias means that you apply what you learn. Don't simply hear and forget what others tell you. Truly listen and appropriately apply the new insight you learn to your new ministry. "Effective leaders strike the right balance between doing (making things happen) and being (observing and reflecting)."[40] One leader reflected over his onboarding experience with these words: "There's a balance between listening and learning, and when to stop listening and take action."[41]

If you listen to others, the grapevine in your church will work on your behalf. As I interviewed people in the first few months, several told me that the church people believed that I was truly listening to them. When people feel heard, and genuine listening helps them feel heard, your influence will deepen and helps create an environment for lasting change.

One caution, though. Be careful about putting too much weight in what you hear from one person. Some disgruntled people may seek you out in your first few days to unduly influence you. Guard yourself against weighing what one or two people say. You'll want to look for patterns and an appreciative inquiry (chapter 6) to help average out extremes to give you a more accurate composite picture.

---

40 Watkins, *Your First 90 Days*, p. 48.

41 Neff and Citrin, *You're in Charge, Now What?*, Kindle e-book loc. 2802.

Your goal in listening is to deepen your understanding of your new ministry by gathering information, analyzing it, and creating next-step action plans based on what you learn.

Listening brings many benefits. We pay others a high compliment when we listen. We affirm their God-given value when we listen. We develop our own heart when we listen. The father of the field of listening, Ralph Nichols, captures the essence of listening in these words. *The most basic of all human needs is the need to understand and be understood. The best way to understand people is to listen to them.*

Several years ago, I received training on how to coach others. The most valuable lessons I learned were these four levels of listening. As you read the four levels below, ask yourself at which level you usually listen.

Level 1 – Listening TO...internal listening. When we listen to others at this level, we mostly listen to our inner dialogue, our thoughts, our feelings, and what we plan to say once the other person has finished speaking. We focus on ourselves, our conclusions, our thoughts about the person/subject of conversation, and what the subject means to us. Unfortunately, most listening happens at this level, where it's mostly about us.

Level 2 – Listening FOR...focused listening. At this level, we begin to authentically listen as we focus on what the other person is saying. We lock onto their dialogue and suppress our temptation to correct, give our opinion, give advice, or offer another perspective as soon as they finish. We become truly present and give them the gift of being understood.

Level 3 – Listening WITH... intuitive listening. At this level, we pay attention to what is not being said through these cues: inflection, pauses, changes in tone and energy, the eyes, and body language. We listen with our gut and allow intuition to speak to our soul.

Level 4 – Listening to the Holy Spirit. This is the deepest level where we intersect what the person is saying/not saying with an openness to what the Spirit of God is saying to us. This level requires great discipline and focus yet provides pastors and ministry leaders a way to become conduits of God's grace to people.

If you prioritize both sides of information flow, avidly overcommunicating *and* listening and learning, you will build a healthy foundation for successful onboarding. In the next chapter, we'll delve into the last part of the PALM acronym, "M," *Manage Change Wisely*.

————

Onboarding tips from an expert: David Self, Executive Pastor at Houston's First Baptist Church, www.houstonsfirst.org

- *The best thing a new ministry leader/pastor can do during the first six months in a new church job*: Learn the history and culture of the church. Often this can be accomplished by simply taking members out for coffee and listening to their stories. Intentionality also allows you to introduce yourself on your terms rather than being defined by hearsay. One doesn't get a second chance to make a good first impression.
- *The dumbest thing David ever heard a pastor do the first six months in a new church job:* He trashed the former pastor and staff, instituting change simply to demonstrate authority to do so. Change without a clear picture of a preferable future simply causes resentment and resistance.

Pause and reflect question: How would your spouse or best friend rate how well you listen?

Next-step application: Take a few moments and list the groups or individuals with whom you must communicate. Jot down some ways you could communicate with them more effectively.

CHAPTER 3

MANAGE CHANGE WISELY

People don't resist change. They resist being changed!
— Peter Senge

⌒

Chapter snapshot:

Prioritize self and family care
Avidly overcommunicate
Listen and learn
Manage change wisely

Poorly managed change will derail healthy onboarding. Well-managed change, however, can smooth the transitions you hope to make in your new ministry. Five change management mindsets can help you maximize how effectively you manage change:

1. Communication
2. Resistance to change
3. Empathy
4. Personality
5. Pace

I'll never forget my first experience at Willow Creek Community Church in Chicago (one of the world's largest churches) several years ago. I had paid the conference fee and booked my plane fare to attend what at the time was Willow's flagship church growth conference. I approached it with trepidation and excitement. I had heard about their success, and I wanted that same success for my new church.

I was a few years into my church plant near Atlanta, Georgia in the then-fastest-growing county in the United States, Gwinnett County. We had just built our first building, Model M-180 in the Southern Baptist denomination architect's book of church building plans. We went with the stretch version so we could seat more. It seated a whopping 150, including kids, when I attended the conference.

On the plane trip there, I convinced myself that I was only a few more good ideas away from my church becoming the Willow of the south. We were poised for growth, rapid growth, or so I thought.

At the conference, I took copious notes as I marveled at their facility and their success. The speakers spoke with deep conviction and inflamed my passion for the church that they coined "the hope of the world." On the flight back, I began to compose what would become my infamous "Willow" sermon that I'd deliver to the church a few weeks later. I outlined the incredible possibilities that loomed before us, which would require immediate and drastic changes to how we currently did ministry.

Over the next few weeks and months, I forced those changes with little regard for the impact on the people. The result? We lost nearly one hundred people during the next twelve months. My change efforts flopped.

In my zeal to grow our church, I had failed to properly manage and communicate change and failed to include others in the process. The church paid a great price and so did I. It took years to regain momentum, and the church never became the "Willow" of the south. Some things certainly needed to change, but in my naivety and passion, I had tried to force change too fast.

***

In your new role, people will expect you to bring change. Yet many of those changes they expect probably don't align with the changes you hope to bring. Nevertheless, they do expect some things to be different. What is the key to successful change? Manage it wisely. The decisions you make early on will "label you as either rash or purposeful, firm or indecisive.... The impression you make and signals you send will either motivate people to pledge their loyalty or allow them to sit on the sidelines, or worse, impel them to turn against you."[42] That's what this chapter is all about...how to bring wise, healthy change and avoid unnecessary collateral damage.

I've listed below the five key change management concepts that I cover in this chapter. These concepts relate to fundamental *mindsets* to understand and develop to bring a healthy change in your new role and deal less with the *specifics* on how to actually create change. A Google search will reveal many books on the how-tos of change. However, one specific change concept is so crucial that I've devoted an entire chapter to it, *Define Reality* (chapter 6).

Here are the five change management mindsets.

- Communicate well what you intend to change, building upon the prior chapter's content.
- Understand why people resist change.
- Recognize that different personalities respond to change in different ways.
- Empathize with those who may resist and fear your changes.
- Discern the appropriate pace and degree of change.

Communicate Well What You Intend to Change

In the last chapter, I emphasized the need to avidly overcommunicate. Successful change management requires this as well. Consider these tips on how to maximize what you communicate about the changes you hope to implement:

---

42   Neff and Citrin, *You're in Charge, Now What?*, Kindle e-book loc. 160.

Keep Those Affected by Your Changes Informed

Schedule when you plan to communicate both the changes and the progress of the changes you are implementing. Bring as many of the players into the conversation as is feasible. Make them feel like insiders. If you make people feel like insiders, they will more readily embrace change.[43] And if your change process is not going as planned, be honest about that, yet focus on solutions without dwelling on problems.

Elicit Feedback from Several Sources about Your Change Plans and Progress

The more collaborative your process, the more successful your change.[44] If others feel they own the change, they're more likely to embrace it. Try to delegate components of your change to others to provide ownership. Also, provide a feedback loop. Give people in your church or ministry a real, tangible way to give you feedback about the changes. When people feel that they both have the opportunity to communicate their thoughts and feel that you will really listen, their anxiety about the future will decrease.

Acknowledge the Change Is Scary for You Too

Don't inadvertently convey that change is difficult for others but not for you. Acknowledge your fears. In doing so, you communicate empathy, which I discuss in more detail later.

Use Narrative Persuasion

In my last book, *Brain-Savvy Leaders, the Science of Significant Ministry*, I explained narrative persuasion this way:

---

43 David Rock, "SCARF in 2012: Updating the Social Neuroscience of Collaborating with Others. Neuroleadership Journal," *Neuroleadership Journal* 4 (2012).

44 Manuel London and James W. Smither, "Can Multi-Source Feedback Change Perceptions of Goal Accomplishment, Self-Evaluations, and Performance-Related Outcomes? Theory-Based Applications and Directions for Research," *Personnel Psychology* 48, no. 4 (1995): 803–839, https://doi.org/10.1111/j.1744-6570.1995.tb01782.x.

Narrative persuasion is a technique that uses indirect communication through story and example. Often, we try to persuade others with a direct approach that communicates just the facts, like, "We are going to make a change, and here are the reasons why." The direct approach often is not effective.

Neuroscientists have confirmed that storytelling has a powerful effect on behavior.[45] Storytelling helps others "see" through the eyes of another. As you solicit feedback, look for stories of people who are managing the change well. Tell their stories as you give updates about your progress. When your team members can see successful responses to change through stories of others, it will help them navigate the change better.[46]

Persuade with Head, Heart, and Hands

Nehemiah, one of the greatest biblical leaders of all time, created change by motivating the people to rebuild the walls around Jerusalem. He used a model for persuasion similar to what Aristotle taught. He said that successful persuasion required three elements: logos, persuasion through reasoning and logic; pathos, persuasion by appealing to emotions; and ethos, persuasion through the force of character or personality.

In Nehemiah 5, after he faced opposition from without (criticism from his adversaries) and opposition from within (discouraged people), he faced a new crisis. The wealthy were exploiting the poor by charging excessive interest rates. As a result, the poor faced hunger, crippling debt, and even slavery because some were forced to sell their children into slavery to pay off the debts.

---

45   Emily B. Falk et al., "Predicting Persuasion-Induced Behavior Change from the Brain," *The Journal of Neuroscience: The Official Journal of the Society for Neuroscience* 30, no. 25 (June 23, 2010): 8421–24, https://doi.org/10.1523/JNEUROSCI.0063-10.2010.

46   Stone, *Brain-Savvy Leaders,* Kindle e-book locs. 2746-2752.

In the midst of that crisis, Nehemiah engaged those three essentials (logos, pathos, and ethos) that prompted the guilty party to change. The rich repented of their abuse and paid back the money they had taken from the poor. He effected the change he sought.

He engaged these three parts of himself to bring that change:

His heart: he engaged his passion (pathos). In verse 6 he writes, *When I heard their outcry and these charges, I was very angry.* In other words, this issue gripped his heart. It stirred his passion and emotions and motivated him to action.

His head: he carefully thought (logos). Rather than reacting to the situation and letting his emotion override good judgment, verse 7 says, *I pondered them in my mind....* In other words, he paused long enough to get a clear picture of things before he acted. James reminds of this when he writes, *My dear brothers, take note of this: Everyone should be quick to listen, slow to speak and slow to become angry, for man's anger does not bring about the righteous life that God desires* (James 1:19-20 NIV).

His hands: he did something (ethos). He showed himself credible through the example he set. Nehemiah didn't just expect others to change. He, too, took responsibility for change by setting a good example. He personally sacrificed by refusing the king's food allotment usually given to governors like himself (vv. 14-16). He committed to never exploit the people as the former leaders had. He committed to *being* a different kind of leader.

Nehemiah wisely managed change by using *his heart, his head, and his hands* to effect that change.

Understand Why People Resist Change

Change is both a scary and a hopeful word. It's scary in that it seems that many church people seem to often oppose it. It's hopeful because all living things change, and we want our churches to be fully alive. Awareness of how our brains work can help you more successfully bring about the changes you want. People resist or embrace your changes largely based on unconscious factors, because the brain tends to interpret change as a threat, which, in turn, creates resistance. The brain is organized around a fundamental principle: *Minimize threat-maximize reward,*[47] which results in either resistance to change or openness to it. The uncertainty of change feels like a threat, which engages the brain's fear centers and creates resistance to change.

God wired our brains for us to seek reward and certainty in our lives. When the future feels ambiguous or uncertain, we subconsciously feel threatened, which creates an *away* response (avoid that which threatens us) that results in resistance. On the other hand, we are drawn toward safety, reward, and pleasure, what cognitive neuroscientists called a *toward* response.

Away responses from people include negativity, fear, passive aggression, or complaining. *Toward* responses might include excitement, support, and good gossip, how we hope people will respond. The more uncertain and ambiguous church change appears, the less support you'll get and the more difficult the change will become. So what do we need to remember so that our changes feel less ambiguous, uncertain, or threatening? Consider these brain-based insights:

Uncertainty Causes People to Fill in Their Knowledge Gaps with Fearful Thoughts

Because uncertainty engages the brain's fear centers, people don't think as clearly when fear is in control. Fear causes more blood, and thus oxygen (the brain's fuel), to flow to our brain's emotional centers (the limbic system) and from our brain's thinking center (the pre-frontal cortex). Because the brain is biased toward negative thinking, people will fill in their information gaps about your change with assumptions that tend to be negative. So the less information you provide, the more people will fill in those gaps with incorrect, fear-based assumptions. As a result, they will become more resistant to change.

---

47   Gordon, E., Barnett, K. J., Cooper, N. J., Tran, N., & Williams, L. M. (2008).
      An "Integrative Neuroscience" Platform: Application to Profiles of Negativity and
      Positivity Bias. *Journal of Integrative Neuroscience, 7*(3), 354–366.

People tend to underestimate their ability to weather difficult future events,[48] and change is usually seen as difficult. Uncertainty causes us to poorly forecast how well we can face the difficulties that change might bring. The concept is called "affective forecasting." When you present change, often others will initially assume that life will be worse for them due to the change. As James Belasco and Ralph Stayer, authors of *Flight of the Buffalos*, wrote, "Change is hard because people overestimate the value of what they have and underestimate the value of what they may gain by giving that up." Keep in mind that people tend to initially latch onto the potential negatives of your change initiative rather than onto the positives.

You Don't Have a Second Chance to Make a Good First Impression

When people first hear about your change, they will tend to draw an initial impression. The quaint saying that *we don't have a second chance to make a good first impression* is more than folklore. Science backs it up.[49] Make sure from day one you commit to clear and hopeful communication. The week I wrote this chapter, I blundered when I introduced a team in our church that would guide our long-range planning process. Some people drew a wrong impression about the team's purpose. Once I realized this, I quickly created an insert for the following Sunday's bulletin to clarify the team's mandate and hopefully decrease resistance to the team's ultimate findings.

Emotions Influence Receptivity to Change

As leaders, we'd prefer that everyone think logically. However, emotions profoundly affect perception, judgment, and thinking. If you simply present

---

48 Timothy D. Wilson and Daniel T. Gilbert, "Affective Forecasting," *Current Directions in Psychological Science* 14, no. 3 (2005): 131–34.

49 Lount, R. B., Zhong, C.-B., Sivanathan, N., & Murnighan, J. K. (2008). Getting Off on the Wrong Foot: The Timing of a Breach and the Restoration of Trust. *Personality and Social Psychology Bulletin, 34*(12), 1601–1612. https://doi.org/10.1177/0146167208324512.

facts about your change without engaging positive and hopeful emotions, your change effort will suffer.

The Human Brain Can Handle Only So Much Change at Once

If you try to create too much change at once, information overload can cause people's fear centers to further activate and resist change.[50] As I noted earlier, when people fear, they don't think as clearly. Make sure you spread out your change initiatives over time rather than pushing too many changes at once.

Old Habits Die Hard

The older we get, we more easily default to what we know. It's like a river that for many years has cut a deep gorge in the earth. It would be hard to change its course. Likewise, older people find it harder to think about other options. Our brain's habit centers get less flexible as we age. It's like a tug-of-war between the familiar and easy (what we are used to, our habits) and the unfamiliar and difficult (the change). But older people can still change if you help them understand the *why* of change and if you communicate clearly (and, of course, if they really want to change). I've had to keep this in mind at my church because we have a large seniors' group.

Resistance to Change Often Increases the Closer You Get to the Actual Change

People's response to change actually changes over time. Let's say you introduce a change that will take place a year from now (you plan to go to two services in your church). Initially, people may see the benefits of another service, such as the flexibility more service time options offers. They probably won't consider the negatives as much like needing more volunteer ushers and children's workers. When the change lies farther into the future, positive feelings usually outstrip negative feelings.[51] However, as the change

---

50 Paul Hemp, "Death by Information Overload - Harvard Business Review," Harvard Business Review, September 2009, http://hbr.org/2009/09/death-by-information-overload/ar/1.

51 Andreas Löw et al., "Both Predator and Prey: Emotional Arousal in Threat and Reward," *Psychological Science* 19, no. 9 (September 2008): 865–73, https://doi.org/10.1111/j.1467-9280.2008.02170.x.

gets closer, people tend to think more about the negative implications and get more fearful. The cost of the change seems more real then, whereas the positives seemed more real early on. The closer you get to implementing change, expect more resistance because uninformed optimism will give way to informed pessimism. Consider how to accentuate the positives the closer you get to your change.

Minimize Cognitive Dissidence

Cognitive dissonance is the inner tension we feel when our beliefs conflict with our behavior (i.e., I want to lose weight but I'm eating a bag of Cheetos) or with new information. Cognitive dissonance creates anxiety that can make us less open to change. One way to help minimize it is to preach and teach to help change people's beliefs about the change you're proposing. If you can help them agree that the reason for the change is biblical (i.e., reach more people by starting a second service), you can help them shift their thinking to align more with a change they must make (i.e., their willingness to sacrifice convenient parking during a renovation). Behavior change tends to follow a change in belief.

Account for the Sunk Cost Bias

Change efforts demand our time, energy, and often our financial resources. Hopefully, people see the benefits your changes will bring. Often, however, the changes will mean people have to give up something they've invested themselves in. When they've already invested considerable time and energy into something, stopping or changing it may seem foolish.

Unfortunately, we tend not to ask ourselves if we really should *continue* investing in a project or ministry. A subtle mental trap comes into play called the *sunk cost bias,* a concept that explains why it's hard to stop something we've invested significant time and energy into. We feel that if we quit, we'd waste what we've already invested and be a failure, even though we should cut our losses and redirect our efforts. When seeking to effect change, recognize that people may have invested in what you hope to change and their emotional connection to it may increase their resistance to the change. Cueing into emotional attachments from the sunk cost bias can help you discover potential pockets of resistance.

Recognize That Different Personalities Respond to Change in Different Ways

Right Brain Avoid or Left Brain Approach?

Our brains process motivation in different ways. One study about motivating people to floss their teeth discovered that different sides of the brain lit up in a scanner (the part of the brain activated) depending on how the message was communicated.[52] If a person was more motivated to *avoid* certain negative things (i.e., floss to avoid bad breath), avoidance type messages motivated them to floss more often. For those motivated more by an *approach* personality (i.e., if I do such-and-such, I will get something good: floss to get great breath), approach messages motivated them to floss more often. People more influenced by their left brain tend to be motivated more by *approach* messages and those influenced more by their right brain by *avoid* messages.[53]

Your church includes both left-brain leaning and right-brain leaning people, so you'll want to include both avoid and approach messages in your change communication plan.

Why or How?

Not only does your church or ministry include both avoid and approach leaning people, but it includes people who want to get information

---

52 David K. Sherman, Traci Mann, and John A. Updegraff, "Approach/Avoidance Motivation, Message Framing, and Health Behavior: Understanding the Congruency Effect," *Motivation and Emotion* 30, no. 2 (June 2006): 165–69, https://doi. org/10.1007/s11031-006-9001-5.

53 Elliot T. Berkman, "Goals, Motivation and the Brain," Psychology Today, November 12, 2012, http://www.psychologytoday.com/blog/the-motivated-brain/201211/goals-motivation-and-the-brain.

in different ways. Some people want to know the *whys* of change related to abstract motivation.[54] Others prefer answers to the *how* of change related to concrete actions.[55] In other words, your messaging should answer two questions: Why do we need to change, and how are we going to change? Some will need more motivation (the why) and some will need more information (the how).

Empathize with Those Who May Resist and Fear Your Changes

Neuroscientists have discovered that the part of our brain directly behind our forehead helps us empathize with others, that is, step into their shoes to see life from their perspective. The process is called mentalizing. It's one way we perceive and intuit the emotions, motivations, and intentions of others in terms of our own thoughts and feelings. Mentalizing is not mind reading. Rather, it's an ability God has given us to perceive another's perspectives better and imagine and interpret their needs, desires, feelings, and goals. The changes you want to bring may make total sense to you but may not to others. Seek to understand how others may perceive your proposed changes and how those changes might affect them. Questions like these can help you empathize, understand their misgivings, and, in turn, know how to address those concerns.

- What emotions could others be feeling about the changes?
- What practical concerns about the changes might they have?
- What do they fear they might lose with the changes?
- What might be their biggest objections to the changes?

Ask key people these questions rather than guessing how they might answer them. Try to create an environment where people feel safe to discuss

---

54 Michel Desmurget and Angela Sirigu, "A Parietal-Premotor Network for Movement Intention and Motor Awareness," *Trends in Cognitive Sciences* 13, no. 10 (October 2009): 411–19, https://doi.org/10.1016/j.tics.2009.08.001.

55 Emily S. Cross et al., "Dissociable Substrates for Body Motion and Physical Experience in the Human Action Observation Network," *European Journal of Neuroscience* 30 (2009): 1383–92.

change with you. When people feel safe around you, you'll help foster the *toward* responses we discussed above. And when that happens, people actually become more open to change.[56]

Discern the Appropriate Pace and Degree of Change

As I mentioned earlier, the brain can only process a limited amount of change at once. Because of that, you'll want to carefully think about pace—how fast or slow you bring change—and degree—how much change you want to effect.

In one church where I was the lead pastor, I approached change too slowly. A few leaders shared their frustration because they thought I was dragging my feet. In my mind, I was setting the stage for change. But in retrospect, I failed to communicate my thinking, which led them to conclude I was dragging my feet. On the other hand, after I attended the Willow Creek conference that I mentioned earlier, I tried to bring too much change too soon. Neff and Citrin capture the importance of appropriate pace and degree with these words. "Just remember that too much change can break the culture—or more likely destroy the change-maker. You have to pace yourself and continually assess the tolerance of the organization."[57]

The expectations you set for the people play a role here as well. Since uncertainty can breed fear and resistance, the more clearly you set expectations, the less uncertainty will work against you. Don't overpromise nor underpromise. Ideally, your church or ministry will see that the benefits of the change will exceed their expectations. When that happens, people become even more willing to embrace future changes. Dr. David Rock, a noted expert on neuroscience and leadership, wrote, "What you expect is what you experience."[58] In other words, expectations can profoundly influence people's experiences.

---

56 Jim Whiting et al., "Lead Change with the Brain in Mind," *Neuroleadership Journal*, no. 4 (2012): 1–15.

57 Neff and Citrin, *You're in Charge, Now What?* Kindle e-book loc 2827.

58 Rock, *Your Brain at Work,* Kindle e-book loc. 2336.

In Chapter 9, *Establish Trust*, I explain why gaining some quick wins is crucial. Early on, it's important that you make changes that will enhance your credibility and address burning issues. But doing it too fast or too slow can hinder effective change, as can trying to change too much or not enough. Although the church or ministry will expect you to bring change, be careful about pushing it until you know the culture, can bring your leaders onboard, and have created a clear change plan. You want to show visible movement during your first six months without wrecking things or losing support or credibility.

***

Change never comes easy, but it's necessary for progress. John F. Kennedy the thirty-fifth president of the United States, once said, "Change is the law of life and those who look only to the past or present are certain to miss the future." And organizational behavioral experts Kenneth Thompson and Fred Luthans noted that a person's reaction to organizational change "can be so excessive and immediate, that some researchers have suggested it may be easier to start a completely new organization than to try to change an existing one."[59] So unless you are starting a new church, recognize the obstacles to change that every leader faces in an existing church. Manage your change wisely with these five mindsets, and God will honor your efforts.

One final note. During the first few months, assuming you have a honeymoon phase (that time period when people's view of you is untainted and mostly positive), your authority to act is based more on your position than on the results you've achieved. People will expect you to bring change and tend to be most open in the beginning. But again, don't push change too fast or you might prematurely shorten your honeymoon.

---

59   Walter McFarland, "This Is Your Brain on Organizational Change," *Harvard Business Review*, October 16, 2012, https://hbr.org/2012/10/this-is-your-brain-on-organizational-change.

You can download a helpful *Change Management Checklist*∞ at the website that gives the five change management mindsets in one place.

Thus far in *Section I*, I've unpacked the four foundational practices required for successful onboarding reflected in the acronym **PALM.**

- **P**rioritize Self and Family Care
- **A**vidly Overcommunicate
- **L**isten and Learn
- **M**anage Change Wisely

Now in *Section II*, I explain a six-step process, **SADDLE**, to apply during your onboarding the first six months in your new ministry. In the next chapter, I unpack the first step, *Start Early.*

———

Onboarding tips from an expert: Darin Yates, executive pastor at Crossroads Church, Cincinnati, www.crossroads.net/media/authors/darin-yates

- *The best thing a new ministry leader can do during the first six months:* The best advice given to me when I started in full-time ministry was to make no changes to systems for at least six months and to make sure my disciplines and relationship with God come first. One mentor told me, "Your first ninety days in ministry will determine how long you'll be able to persevere in ministry. If you try to make an immediate impact at the expense of your relationship with God, you will accomplish short-term results because you are smart and hard-working. Yet those results will likely fade quickly. If you prioritize your time with God, you'll likely still make an impact, but it will be a sustainable one."
- *The dumbest thing Darin has ever heard that a pastor did the first six months:* The biggest mistakes I see often, particularly

with young pastors, is they want to restructure their team immediately. This is almost always a mistake. You don't know enough about the church, the team, God's desires for the team, or the team culture to make wise choices early. Resist this temptation.

Pause and reflect question: How well have you handled change in previous ministries?

Next-step application: Reflect over a change in a previous ministry that didn't go well. Given what you know now, what would you have done differently? Write down two or three general principles that you could apply in a future change you hope to bring in your new ministry.

CHAPTER 4

START EARLY

Success or failure during the first few months is a strong predictor
of overall success or failure in (a) job.[60]
— Michael D. Watkins

⌒

Chapter snapshot:

Start early
Avoid common pitfalls
Define reality
Develop a game plan
Lead your team
Establish trust

This phase in the onboarding process, if implemented before day one, can set the stage for a healthy start in your new ministry role. It includes these six steps:

1. Know yourself.
2. Do your due diligence.

---

60   Watkins, *The First 90 Days,* Kindle e-book loc 139.

> 3. Manage your pre-hiring firsts.
> 4. Leave your current ministry well.
> 5. Rest up.
> 6. Get a head start.

Why Start Early?

In the letter to the church at Corinth, the Apostle Paul paralleled the Christian life to an athlete running a race (1 Cor 9). And of course, all athletes want to win their races. They know they can't win a race without prior preparation. The same holds true for your move into your new ministry. Jesus Himself reminded us about preparing ourselves before we make a significant decision when he explained what it meant to follow Him: *Suppose one of you wants to build a tower. Will he not first sit down and estimate the cost to see if he has enough money to complete it?* (Luke 14:28 NIV).

Unfortunately, a fallacy into which many pastors fall is this thinking: "The first day of my ministry starts on the first day I'm in the office." I fell into such thinking in my early ministries. I subconsciously assumed that since the paycheck didn't start until my first day, I should not yet be working. In reality, though, if you want to get a good start, view your job as starting the moment a new church considers you a candidate. I believe two crucial phases precede day one: the time before you receive an offer and the time between your acceptance and your first day on the job. Neff and Citrin offered this advice:

> The days leading up to the point when you actually take the job are some of the most important to being successful. Day one on the job better not be day one where you're working on your action plan; it should be well under way by the time you get there.[61]

View this time period as a gift that will allow you to carefully consider your decision, get ahead, jump start your learning, and accomplish some

---

61   Neff and Citrin, *You're in Charge-Now What?*, Kindle e-book loc. 317.

critical tasks that will free up time during the hectic first few weeks on the job. The authors of *The New Leader's 100-Day Action Plan* call this phase the "fuzzy front end," the bonus time or white space before day one in the office. They note, "New leaders who miss the opportunity to get a head start before the start often discover later that organizational ... momentum was working against them even before they showed up for their first full day at the office."[62]

In the pages that follow I'll explain the first letter in the S.A.D.D.L.E. strategy, *Start Early*, as I suggest six steps that encompass it.

Step 1: Know Yourself

The ancient Greek aphorism, *Know Thyself*, captures the essence of this step. John Calvin expanded upon this idea with these words, "Nearly all wisdom we possess, that is to say, true and sound wisdom, consists in two parts: the knowledge of God and of ourselves."[63] So the better you know yourself, the better your ability to discern whether or not this prospective role would fit who you are. John Piper, well-known pastor-author penned these words when he took eight months off from his role as lead pastor.

Pastors, you will know your people's souls best by knowing your own. So try to be ruthlessly honest with yourself. The key here is not professionalism. The best soul-searcher and the best counselor may have no letters after their names. The key is brutal, broken vulnerability and honesty, sustained by pleas for mercy, and soaked in the riches of Scripture—both its warnings and its wonders.[64]

---

62 George B. Bradt, Jayme A. Check, and Jorge E. Pedraza, *The New Leader's 100-Day Action Plan: How to Take Charge, Build Your Team, and Get Immediate Results*, 3 edition (Hoboken, N.J: Wiley, 2011), Kindle Locations 2412.

63 John Calvin, *Institutes of the Christian Religion*, Revised edition (Peabody, Mass: Hendrickson Publishers, Inc., 2007), Kindle e-book loc. 757.

64 John Piper, "Pastor, Know Thyself," Leadership Journal, February 11, 2013, https://www.christianitytoday.com/pastors/2013/february-online-only/pastor-know-thyself.html.

What should you do to know yourself as you consider a new role? I suggest that you reflect upon seven *know yourself* areas as you seek to discern God's will. You can download the *Know Yourself Matrix*∞ tool, where you can put all seven of these in one place to visualize a composite picture of how you are wired.

1. Your spiritual gifts
2. Your emotional intelligence
3. Your personality style
4. Your leadership style
5. Your true north values
6. Your entry style
7. Your anxiety bias

In the paragraphs that follow, I unpack some of the *know yourself* areas. For others, I mostly recommend resources you can consult for a fuller understanding.

Your Spiritual Gifts

I assume most pastors understand spiritual gifts. Key biblical passages on gifts include Romans 12, 1 Corinthians 12, and Ephesians 4. If you don't know your gifts, study these passages and ask those close to you what gifts they believe you have. www.gifttest.org offers a helpful inventory that may help you discern your unique spiritual gifts.

Your Emotional Intelligence

Emotional intelligence (EQ) is "the capacity of individuals to recognize their own, and other people's emotions, to discriminate between different feelings and label them appropriately, and to use emotional information to guide thinking and behavior."[65] Dr. Daniel Goleman popularized this term in the 1990s with his book *Emotional Intelligence*. EQ indicates strengths or

---

65   Andrew M. Colman, *A Dictionary of Psychology*, 4 edition (Oxford: Oxford University Press, 2015).

weaknesses in four areas: two around personal competence (self-awareness and self-management) and two around social competence (social awareness and relationship management). I recommend that every ministry leader take an EQ inventory and seek to improve their EQ. You can find many free inventories online. However, I recommend that you purchase the book *Emotional Intelligence 2.0* by Travis Bradberry and Jean Greaves, which includes a link to a statistically valid online assessment. The assessment and the book also provide practical tips on how to improve your EQ. Understanding how well you recognize and manage your and other's emotions can greatly enhance your ability to onboard well.

Your Personality Style

For years, churches, organizations, and individuals have used personality style insight to improve leadership and relationships. I recommend Ministry Insights' *Leading from Your Strengths* profile, available at their website. Another good tool, the *StrengthsFinder Profile*, helps you understand your unique leadership strengths. You can find a link for this profile by purchasing the book by Marcus Buckingham and Donald O. Clifton, *Now, Discover Your Strengths: How to Build Your Strengths and the Strengths of Every Person in Your Organization*.

Your Leadership Style

Although founder and former pastor of Willow Creek Community Church, Bill Hybels, has faced some difficult times, he's written many helpful books on leadership. In his book *Courageous Leadership: Field-Tested Strategy for the 360° Leader*, he describes ten kinds of leaders. I've summarized them below. Read Hybels's book to further understand these styles.

1. *Visionary leader.* This leader casts vision well because he can clearly see what needs to happen. Their faith fuels future-oriented idealism.
2. *Directional leader.* These leaders embody great wisdom to point their organization in the right direction. They can articulate values, mission, strengths, and weaknesses well.

3. *Strategic leader.* This leader can distill vision into achievable steps to create an understandable game plan that invites the participation of others.

4. *Managing leader.* This kind of leader can establish destination milestones and then achieve the mission as they organize and monitor people, processes, and resources.

5. *Motivational leader.* These leaders know who they need to challenge or train, and they know how to say and do the right things to motivate others.

6. *Shepherding leader.* These people love their team members and show it through their genuine support and prayer, which helps the organization achieve its mission.

7. *Team-building leader.* These leaders can develop others into cohesive teams with complementary competencies, character, and chemistry. They know how to put people in the right positions for the right reasons to produce the right results.

8. *Entrepreneurial leader.* These leaders function well in start-up settings and embody personal energy, vision, and a risk-taking spirit.

9. *Re-engineering leader.* This leader thrives in organizations that have lost their way. They can assess what the mission was, what it needs to be, and how to measure progress to get where it needs to go.

10. *Bridge-building leader.* This person brings a wide variety of people together under a single umbrella so that an organization can be successful. Such a leader shows great flexibility with these skills: negotiation, healthy compromise, listening, and thinking outside the box.

Your True North Values

Every leader should be clear on what I call *true north values*. Such values aren't the essential values every Christian leader should embrace, like keeping the ten commandments, obeying the golden rule, or living out Jesus' great command and great commission. Rather, they reflect more nuanced values that capture the essence of the real you deep in your soul. These values should infuse your soul and leadership so that nothing external could cause you to compromise them. Granted, they might be aspirational and not yet fully developed. Nevertheless, they describe the authentic, Christ-honoring You to which you aspire. You can download a step-by-step tool to help you discover your values called the *How to Discover Your True North Values Retreat Plan∞* as well as a list of my true north values called *Charles Stone's True North Values∞* to give an example of what they look like.

Your Entry Style

Roy M. Oswald, author of *New Beginnings, A Pastorate Start-Up Workbook,*[66] encourages pastors considering a new church to become familiar with what he calls their entry style. He writes that each of us has a consistent pattern in how we engage and disengage other people in daily life. Those patterns will carry over into a new ministry setting. These basic principles underlie those styles.[67]

- They are often unconscious.
- They are so deeply embedded that permanently changing them is difficult to do, although we can temporarily change them.
- Those patterns tend to be consistent in brief relationship encounters as well as in long-term relationships like marriage.

When you begin to interact with search teams, staff, volunteers, and church people in your prospective role, you will tend to act in the same way you did in your previous ministry. It's important to understand how you actually and unconsciously relate to people when you first meet them. Ask a close friend to share with you what he or she observes when you meet

---

66   Roy M. Oswald, *New Beginnings: A Pastorate Start Up Workbook* (Washington, DC: Rowman & Littlefield Publishers, 1989).

67   Ibid, pp 23-27.

someone for the first time. These questions might help you discover your style and modify it as needed.

- What is my handshake like?
- What kind of eye contact do I usually give?
- What does my body language convey when I listen to others?
- What kind of people am I drawn to?
- What kind of people turn me off?

If you understand your answers to the last two questions, you can avoid inadvertently making people who naturally turn you off feel that you don't like them. We all subconsciously look for subtle clues about how others feel about us and read intentions and emotions. We call this process *mentalizing*. How you relate to the search team and your potential employer in those initial encounters will affect their first (and long-term) impressions of you. If you know your entry style, you can make changes to avoid unnecessary barriers in those first contacts.

Your Anxiety Bias

Stress and anxiety come with ministry, and our bodies and brains respond to stress in various ways. We all have an anxiety bias, a default mode we tend to fall into when under stress and anxiety. This anxiety bias shows up in one or more of these eight responses. As you read this list below, consider which one describes your bias or tendency when under stress.

- *Fight*: emotionally reacting and becoming defensive
- *Flee*: emotionally or physically cutting off from others in anxious situations
- *Freeze*: not knowing what to do, thus not taking a position; offering no opinion and/or staying neutral when you should take a position
- *Fuse*: losing your identity by glomming onto another's wants and desires, compromising convictions, seeking unity at all costs, and/or trying to force everybody to be one big, happy family

- *Fixate*: easily getting sucked into unhealthy relationships and conflict
- *Fix*: overperforming to fix somebody else's problems or doing for others what they should do for themselves
- *Flounder*: becoming passive, underperforming, or giving up
- *Feed/ fornicate/ finances*: inappropriately yielding to base impulses by turning to food, illicit sex/pornography, or inappropriate use of money

When we know our biases, we can draw deeply from God's promises to lessen their pull. Scripture tells us that the Lord has given us everything we need to live a godly life. Second Peter 1:3 encourages us with these words: *His divine power has given us everything we need for life and godliness through our knowledge of him who called us by his own glory and goodness (NIV).*

God has crafted our bodies and brains, our souls and minds, and our regenerated hearts with the capability to cool our emotions and lessen anxiety in the midst of stress. Acting calmly when tempted to do otherwise glorifies him.[68] And when you know how you respond to anxiety, and adjust accordingly, your first experiences in your prospective role will go much better.

As you prepare for your new assignment and those initial contacts, take time to understand yourself. Get clear on your strengths. Get clear on what you do best. Get clear on what you should avoid or change. Knowing yourself takes a lifetime. However, during this potential transition, the more you know yourself, the greater the chance you'll discern if the opportunity fits you, and if it does, your onboarding will go smoother as well.

Step 2. Do Your Due Diligence

In chapter 6, *Define Reality*, I'll explain this concept as it applies to your first few weeks on the job. But in the pre-hiring phase, attempt to

---

68   Charles Stone, *People-Pleasing Pastors: Avoiding the Pitfalls of Approval-Motivated Leadership* (Downers Grove, IL: IVP Books, 2014) Kindle Locations 2415-2432.

understand all you can about the prospective church or ministry, including its history, the ministry role itself, and what the board or your boss expects of you. You probably won't be able to discern what the staff and the church expect until a few weeks after you begin. Nevertheless, you can learn a lot.

The early and obvious places to learn about the potential ministry include the following:

1. *The job posting.* Churches now use the internet to post open positions. You'll want to become familiar with everything on the posting, including the job description. If the posting does not include a job description, you'll want to see one early in the candidating process.

2. *The church's website.* You can learn lots about the church not only from the website content but from the site's look and feel as well. A dated, clunky website conveys one thing. A nice, clean, easy-to-use site conveys something else.

3. *The church's Facebook page.* Does the church have one? Is it current? What insight about the church can you glean from the postings?

4. *A Google search.* Often, you'll find information about the church in other places on the web other than its website.

Although these sources will inform you about the role, well-placed questions during the candidating process will probably tell you the most. You'll most likely experience a tiered interview process beginning with phone or Skype calls. If the church/hiring pastor/hiring agency wants to continue the process, on-site visits usually follow. It's important to create a clear, concise set of questions to ask at each phase of the interview process (see below).

In my case, the interview process included four phone calls with the interim pastor, who was also charged with narrowing the field of candidates. We talked probably six hours total during those calls. He explained the setting and role and asked me questions, and I asked him questions. As the process progressed, I made two visits to Canada, the first involving an extended interview with the elder board. The second visit included sessions with other groups in the church and the church meeting to vote to hire me.

At each phase of the candidating process, I asked deeper and more specific questions. Create your own list within these three groupings based on where you are in the process.

Early questions (first interview): these involve high-level questions to help you better understand the church and its history. At this stage, guard against asking too many questions. Focus primarily on 10,000-foot view type questions.

Mid questions (second phone interview/first live interview): these questions focus on expectations, qualities the prospective board/boss is looking for in the new hire, and how the leadership envisions the church's future.

Late questions (late in the first live interview or during the second live interview with the board/boss; when you think an offer is imminent): these questions include tactical ones like salary and benefits.

Below, I've listed a few key questions I asked at each step in the process. You'll notice that most are opened ended questions that require more than a *yes* or *no* answer. This *Key Hiring Questions*∞ list and another list called *Miscellaneous Hiring Questions*∞ are available for download as well.

Early questions:
1.   What are the church's/ministry's greatest strengths?
2.   How does the community view the church?
3.   What have been the greatest challenges facing the church in recent years?
4.   Is a job description available? (If one has not been posted online or sent to you, ask for a copy.)
5.   Does the church have a constitution and/or bylaws document? Ask for a copy.

6. What are the attendance statistics for the last few years?
7. What are the steps/timeline in the hiring process?

Mid-process questions:

1. What is your dream for the church's future?
2. What stands out as the church's fondest memory?
3. How healthy is the church financially? What is the church's debt? How are financial decisions made? If you are entering a role other than senior pastor, ask how much money is budgeted for your area. Ask for the latest financial statement and annual budget.
4. How are decisions made at the staff and board level?
5. What about my qualities and experience attracted you to me?
6. What are your general expectations of me? My spouse?
7. How tolerant of change is the church? How did the last significant change go? What is off limits for change?
8. How would you describe the staff unity and relationships?
9. Is there a staff organizational chart? Ask for one.
10. What are the core values of the church?

Late-process questions:

1. How would you define my success one, three, and five years out?
2. What were the strengths and weaknesses of the prior person who filled this role?
3. How would you describe the elder board and staff unity and relationships?
4. How does the board relate to the person in this role? How are staff hired and fired? For a helpful tool WestPark created that delineates the pastor-board relationship, you can download *Guiding Principles That Guide Board-Pastor Relationships.*∞
5. Does the church have a staff policy manual that outlines vacation, sick leave, and conference time? Ask for a copy.
6. What is the salary and benefits package (insurance, retirement, etc.)? Is there a book, conference, phone, mileage, etc. allowance?

Don't be afraid to ask these questions late in the process. If the search team or boss hedges on giving you answers to these, consider that a red flag.

7.　What is the salary review process?

Step 3. Manage Well Your Pre-Hiring Firsts

As I covered above, the pre-hiring phase includes several milestones:

- The first email contact
- The first phone/Skype contact
- The second phone/skype contact (or third or fourth or ...)
- The first face-to-face interview
- The second face-to-face interview (or third or fourth or ...)
- The actual offer for employment

If you are married, at some point you will need to include your spouse in the interviews and face-to-face meetings, because your spouse should be a major influencer in your decision. If the church balks at bringing him or her into the process, consider this a red flag.

Throughout this phase, you'll want to maintain a mindset (see chapter 2) to learn as much as you can about this role and the church. You'll also want to put your best foot forward while still being authentic. Also, remember your entry styles mentioned earlier. Behaviors as simple as eye contact and dress can determine the tone of a meeting and how people feel about you. And a firm, confident, friendly handshake can actually calm the fear centers in a stranger's brain and activate the brain's reward centers.[69] So make sure you have a good handshake.

The Offer

If the church wants to hire you, an offer will follow, and you'll want to get all your questions answered about the specifics of the contract. Spend

---

69　Sanda Dolcos et al., "The Power of a Handshake: Neural Correlates of Evaluative Judgments in Observed Social Interactions," *Journal of Cognitive Neuroscience* 24, no. 12 (September 27, 2012): 2292–2305, https://doi.org/10.1162/jocn_a_00295.

significant time praying throughout the entire process. I suggest also that you seek input from those you trust, especially your spouse and your kids. God will honor your due diligence and point you in the right direction.

You may be tempted to take a job simply because you need a job. If this is your first ministry experience, taking a less-than-ideal job for experience might make sense. But if you are further along in your ministry, guard against taking a job just because you need the money. When I candidated at WestPark, several other churches were simultaneously pursuing me. They were in the U.S. and were larger churches. In one, I would have begun as the associate and then moved into the senior role a few years later. At this stage in my ministry and life, that option didn't seem viable. Another church twice the size of WestPark with a strong financial base, a good location, and great facilities also pursued me. But one issue gave me a huge heart check. In conversations with the board chair, he explained that at their elders' meetings, they would dismiss the lead pastor halfway through to discuss further business. Even though the other factors in this church were good, that one issue (keeping the lead pastor out of part of the elder's meetings) prompted me to discontinue that conversation.

Assuming you've now said yes, the *Start Early* phase includes three final steps I briefly cover below.

Step 4. Leave Your Current Ministry Well

Earlier, I wrote about how we must deal with the pain from our prior ministry to be most effective in our new one. But leaving well involves more than processing our pain. In fact, psychologists tell us that we can't open a new chapter in our lives without closing the prior one. It's called closure.[70]

I wrote earlier about how a wave of sadness swept over me the first few weeks during a new role I took when I moved to California. Neither disappointment nor inward anger fueled that grief. Rather, the loss of leaving a church we had built from the ground up did. Loss usually means

---

70   Lauren Suval, "Finding Closure," *Psych Central.com*, accessed March 25, 2016, http://psychcentral.com/blog/archives/2012/06/20/finding-closure/.

that we must grieve at some level. And unless we stay at the same church our entire life, we will leave one ministry or church and go to another, perhaps several times. In fact, Thom Rainer, well-known church growth expert, notes that the average pastor in the U.S. stays at one place only three to four years.[71] At my current church, I hope God will give me at least ten years of fruitful service before my age reminds me that I no longer have the energy for a full-time lead pastoral role.

I've served at six different churches in my thirty-nine years in ministry and have learned the following insights about leaving well and making a graceful exit:

Leave on top. That is, leave your ministry as healthy and as strong as possible. The Apostle Paul challenges us with these words: *Whatever you do, work at it with all your heart, as working for the Lord, not for men…. (Col 3:23 NIV).*

Speak well of your former leaders and church. Don't leave a trail of gossip. Don't undermine the leaders or anyone else there who may have hurt you. Don't burn bridges. Leave in such a way that both your and Christ's reputation remain intact. As the writer of Proverbs reminds us, *A good name is more desirable than great riches; to be esteemed is better than silver or gold. (Prov 22:1 NIV).*

Let go of ownership. Remember, you are no longer in charge at your previous church. You might be tempted to continue influencing it from afar. Resist that temptation.

Pray that God would bless the ministry even more under the new leader who replaces you. When the baton of leadership passed from David to Solomon, the words spoken by one of the priests remind us to pray for God's blessings on those who succeed us: *May the Lord be with Solomon as he has been with you, and may God make Solomon's reign even greater than yours! (1 Kgs 1:37 NIV).*

---

71   "The Dangerous Third Year of Pastoral Tenure," ThomRainer.com, June 18, 2014, http://thomrainer.com/2014/06/dangerous-third-year-pastoral-tenure/.

Syndicated columnist Ellen Goodman captured the spirit of a leader who makes a graceful exit when she wrote the following words on leaving well:

> *There is a trick to the Graceful Exit. It begins with the vision to recognize when a job, a life stage, a relationship is over—and let it go. It means leaving what's over without denying its validity or its past importance to our lives. It involves a sense of future, a belief that every exit line is an entry, that we are moving on, rather than out.*[72]

Step 5. Rest Up

Give yourself as much time between the two ministries as is practically and financially feasible. Don't fill up that space only with packing, moving, and unpacking. Rather, build in time to rest and rejuvenate as well. If you can, request more time between leaving your current role and beginning your new one. When we moved to Canada, we took two weeks to settle in even before I went into the office. And I moved into my office a week before I was scheduled to start. Actually, I wish I had asked for another week. Also, ask the search team or your boss to push the public announcement of your arrival a week or so beyond the actual day you begin. I attended the church incognito the first week I was on the field and was able to experience WestPark before everyone knew I had arrived.

Your transition will tire you out more than you think. The more time you can take to refresh yourself and build your internal energy reserve before you start, the better your onboarding will go.

Step 6. Get a Head Start

This final step may seem contradictory to step 5, but it is very important if you can schedule extra time to accomplish some tasks before your start date, in addition to scheduling time to rest. To reiterate, take as

---

72 Seattle Times staff, "Ellen Goodman's Last Column: Looking Backward, Looking Forward," The Seattle Times, January 1, 2010, http://www.seattletimes.com/opinion/ellen-goodmans-last-column-looking-backward-looking-forward/.

much time as you can between ministries. You'll be glad you did.

What are some ways you can get a head start? Every setting is unique, but I've listed below a few steps I took before day one that gave me a good head start:

- I began to outline my six-month game plan, the basic strategy I would follow the first few months at WestPark. In chapter 7 (*Develop a Game Plan*) I explain how to do this.
- I began to identify key people with whom I needed to meet the first month.
- I scheduled some pre-start meetings and attended a few before my start date. I had dinner with an elder and his wife and dinner with the interim and his wife. I attended a lunch meeting with other area pastors. I attended a full elder's meeting as a fly on the wall. I attended the church's annual business meeting. I met with the elder chair and the interim pastor for an emergency meeting concerning a significant staff issue. I attended a staff meeting, and I met with the then-current worship pastor.
- I made several introductory calls.
- I chose my first sermon series and began studying for it.

Get a head start the best you can. Learn as much as you can before you begin. Jumpstart the process so that you began to shape things before they shape you.

In this chapter, we've looked at the six steps crucial to getting a good start, the first phase in the **SADDLE** process, "S" for *Start Early*. In the next chapter, we'll look at the second step, *Avoid Common Pitfalls*, where I describe some hidden risks and challenges you'll want to sidestep.

_____

Onboarding tips from an expert: Ron Baker, lead pastor at VitalPoint Church, London, Ontario (www.vitalpointchurch.com), former executive pastor at Forest City Church, London, Ontario

- *The best thing a new ministry leader can do during the first six months:* Often a new pastor will step into this role with great excitement, ready to impress and impact those they lead, but what happens is they lose sight of who they are and what they have been called to do. In the first six months, they need to establish great routine and rhythms and stick to them. Doing this will help the people understand where they fit into the big picture of the pastor's life. It will be very tough to do because of the demands, but if the pastor can stay strong, they will gain respect and have a greater impact in the long run.
- *The dumbest thing Ron has ever heard that a pastor did the first six months:* The answer comes from my own life. I put the church before my family when our first son was born. I had been a pastor for one month. When our first son was born, I brought them home from the hospital, opened the front door, left them there, and went back to my pastoral duties to assist in a funeral that I didn't really need to be at. I felt I needed to impress the church with my dedication to the "job." I would never do that again in a million years.

Pause and reflect question: In which of the six steps above are you most deficient? Why do you think that's so?

Next-step application: Depending on the stage you're in, with respect to your new role, schedule one hour this week to create an action plan to help you improve yourself in that area.

CHAPTER 5

AVOID COMMON PITFALLS

We are not fit to lead an army on the march unless we are familiar with the
face of the country— its mountains and forests, its pitfalls and precipices,
its marshes and swamps.
— Sun Tzu

⤳

Chapter snapshot:

Start early
Avoid common pitfalls
Define reality
Develop a game plan
Lead your team
Establish trust

Every new role is fraught with pitfalls, often unseen. New ministry leaders will face many pitfalls, but these seven are the most common.

1. *Cookie Cutter: Thinking what worked before will work now*
2. *Smartie-pants: Assuming you know all the answers*
3 *Out of sight, out of mind…NOT!: Failure to recognize the former leader's lingering influence*

> 4   Blindsided: Failure to clarify expectations and prepare for surprises
>
> 5   Fire, ready, aim: Overemphasizing quick results
>
> 6   Scaredy-cat: Risk aversion
>
> 7   People-pleaser: Saying yes to too many things

A quaint story circulated among Methodists describes a young pastor fresh out of seminary who had just begun his first pastorate. As he drove up to the small church, he noticed an old tree blocking the side doors into the building. In his exuberance, he cut the tree down to show the congregation his decisive leadership. Unfortunately, no one told him that they believed that John Wesley, the founder of Methodism, had planted it hundreds of years earlier. He had one of the shortest pastorates on record after that.[73] Even if this story is somewhat dubious, it captures what often happens in a new ministry when a new pastor is blind to potential pitfalls.

Sydney Finkelstein, author and Dartmouth Tuck School of Business professor, conducted a massive study on why leaders fail. His book, *Why Smart Executives Fail*, reveals his research. He explains seven destructive behaviors common to leaders in failing companies.[74] He discovered that the issues we might assume would contribute most to failure, such as dishonesty, wrong motivations, or poor leadership ability weren't the most common factors. Rather, he discovered that soft skills such as self-image, pride, poor communication, a savior complex, and misaligned expectations contributed most to their failure. During the first six months, such land mines often lie hidden to a new leader.

Another onboarding expert writes, "Onboarding is like an organ transplant, and you're the transplanted organ."[75] So if you fall into these

---

73   Angie Best-Boss, *Surviving Your First Year as Pastor: What Seminary Couldn't Teach You* (Valley Forge, PA: Judson Press, 1999), pp xi-xii.

74   Sydney Finkelstein, *Why Smart Executives Fail: And What You Can Learn from Their Mistakes*, Reprint edition (New York: Portfolio, 2004).

75   Watkins, *The First 90 Days*, p. 27.

traps, the new church's immune system could turn on you and reject you.

The Scriptures often remind us to stay alert and avoid pitfalls, potholes, problems, and sin. It tells us to...

- Be prepared for Jesus' return (1 Thess 5).
- Watch for the influence of Satan (1 Pet 5:8).
- Keep our minds ready for action (1 Pet 1:13).
- Maintain a general watchfulness about life through prayer (Col 4:2).
- Be watchful to avoid temptation (Matt 26:40-41).
- Persevere in alertness and prayer (Eph 6:18).
- Stand guard (1 Cor 16:13).

Therefore, it's important to keep in mind these seven pitfalls as I unpack the second letter in the **SADDLE** strategy, "A," for *Avoid Common Pitfalls*.

Pitfall # 1. Cookie cutter: Thinking what worked before will work now

"It's a mistake to believe that you will be successful in your new job by continuing to do what you did in your previous job, only more so."[76] This pitfall reflects a one-size-fits-all approach to ministry. Such thinking not only could be a mismatch for the church but could stifle learning new ways to do ministry crucial to your continued professional and spiritual growth.

Sometimes this pitfall shows up when we realize we're talking too much about our previous ministry and our successes there. An occasional reference to your former ministry is fine. But when it becomes commonplace, your staff, volunteers, and people in the church may hear you imply that your prior ministry was better than your current one. Don't communicate buyer's remorse, even if you feel it.

---

76   Ibid, p. 19.

This was a particularly sensitive issue for me when I moved from the U.S. to Canada. I'd served most of my ministry life in the U.S., and after a year in Canada, I recognized that much of North American ministry philosophy had become U.S. centric. Like fish don't know what life is like out of water until they're out of it, I had to get out of American church culture to see this for myself. I not only had to guard against comparing my current setting to success in my previous churches but also avoid inferring that U.S. churches did ministry better than Canadian churches (which they don't necessarily do). I now believe that as the U.S. becomes more post-Christian, American churches can learn much from Canadian churches.

Pitfall # 2. Smartie-Pants: Assuming you know all the answers

I still remember an embarrassing conversation with a leader in the first church where I was lead pastor. We disagreed on an issue and I recall saying, "I'm usually right on most things." When I think back on that statement, I cringe at the egotism I conveyed. I had failed to remember that Proverbs 16:18 warns that pride comes before a fall.

If those around you sense that you have all the answers, you'll alienate them. Liz Wiseman, author of *Multipliers: How the Best Leaders Make Everyone Smarter*, calls these leaders "accidental diminishers," leaders who, in giving all the answers, actually squelch ideas in others.[77] When that happens, people may withhold important information you need to know in your new leadership role. Getting correct feedback is crucial to successful onboarding, even if it's not what you want to hear. A know-it-all attitude can stifle opposing perspectives you need to hear as a new leader. And failing to seek input from others can also convey a smarty-pants attitude. You don't know what you don't know, and you'll never know it unless you intentionally seek out hidden information.

If you have considerable ministry experience, you may, in fact, be the smartest person in the room at any given moment. But avoid conveying

---

[77] "Are You an Accidental Diminisher? |," accessed May 21, 2019, http://iveybusinessjournal.com/publication/are-you-an-accidental-diminisher/.

that attitude or you'll turn people off and lose support. You'll want to convey a teachable attitude reflected in the "L" of the **PALM** acronym, *listen and learn.*

Pitfall # 3. Out of Sight, Out of Mind…NOT!: Failure to recognize the former leader's lingering influence

Often, people will fondly remember the former leader whose place you just filled, if they were well-liked. When I came to WestPark, the prior pastor had built enduring relationships with many of the seniors, and he came back to perform many of their funerals. I celebrated his doing that. However, in another church where I served as lead pastor, I was not as wise. I share this quote from my book *People-Pleasing Pastors.*

> *I recall one church where I served where the founding pastor had been a father figure to many of the early members. He was "larger than life" from both the stage and in one-on-one relationships. Because many of the old timers had come to faith through his ministry, most had never seen any other pastor lead, except him. He had become close friends with many of the stakeholders. He also had made himself available to them 24-7. The father figure he played loomed large. When I arrived as senior pastor, my leadership style was not to give people 24-7 availability, except in emergencies, because I'd soon burn out if I did. I was also more of a ready-aim-fire leader, whereas he was known as a fire-fire-fire leader.*

> *After about a year, I begin to sense a weird vibe from some of the stakeholder leaders. It seemed that I couldn't please them, no matter what I did. I felt befuddled. But as a clearer picture of this pastor emerged, I began to understand what fueled this tension. I realized that some leaders wanted the best parts of him, in me. They wanted a father figure who was available 24-7. One leader even confessed to me he expected me to be a father to him.*

They loved his larger-than-life dreams that seemed to come "straight from the Holy Spirit." It excited them and many felt that church should be perpetually exciting. My vision, however, came more slowly through a more deliberate and thoughtful process, definitely not eliciting as much emotional excitement as did his. They had transferred the idealized former pastor's strengths onto me, and I had failed to meet those expectations.

Edwin Friedman captured this transference when he noted, "Institutions… tend to institutionalize the pathology, or the genius, of the founding families." [78]

This founding pastor had left under difficult circumstances. As a result, I also bumped into another unspoken script: a fear and distrust for strong pastoral leadership among some stakeholder leaders. Had I known how churches, like families, pass down dysfunctionality, I could have better navigated these bumps. [79]

Failure to realize the former leader's influence is a potential pitfall you want to avoid. Seek out insight from stakeholders about the former leader's strengths, weaknesses, and leadership style. However, avoid giving the perception that you want this information to boost how others view you or that you are criticizing what he did. Rather, communicate to those you ask that such insight can help you serve the church better.

Pitfall # 4. Blindsided: Failure to clarify expectations or prepare for surprises

In chapter 1, I wrote about your family's expectations. Here I use expectations to refer to what your *boss or board* expects from you. If you

---

78   Edwin H. Friedman, *A Failure of Nerve: Leadership in the Age of the Quick Fix* (Bethesda, MD: Friedman Estate, 1999), Kindle e-book loc. 3849.

79   Stone, *People-Pleasing Pastors*, Kindle e-book loc. 1175.

aren't clear on their expectations, even if you think you are performing well in the early days, you may be in for surprise disappointment.

When I came to WestPark, expectations ran high. I felt that as soon as the church voted 100 percent to call me as the lead pastor. That unanimous vote initially created some anxiety in me about the board's expectations. However, because I had asked the right questions in the pre-hiring phase (see the previous chapter), I felt confident I could meet their expectations with the Holy Spirit's help.

In the pre-hiring phase, the better you understand your job description and unwritten expectations, the less unmet expectations will blindside you. Get answers to your questions for anything unclear. Talk to your board or boss to further clarify what they want. After you begin, continue dialogue with them to make sure you continue to understand and meet their expectations. Prioritize healthy communication with them.

Another way to avoid surprises is to avoid setting expectations too high. Guard against making lofty promises you can't keep. It's better to underpromise and overperform. Yet don't set expectations too low, because you may lose the support of some of your high-performing people if they sense you are playing it safe by setting them low. As I wrote in chapter 2 about listening and learning, I set a reasonable expectation to the church that I would listen a lot before I made significant changes.

You will face surprises in those first few months. Clarify expectations early to minimize them. When they come, don't panic. When your enthusiasm and the church's enthusiasm wanes after a few months, which is inevitable when the newness wears off, don't be thrown by that dip. Manage your response with God's power.

Pitfall # 5. Fire, Ready, Aim: Overemphasizing quick results

Sometimes a new leader feels both a compulsion to do something quickly to prove his or her worth and/or takes too much responsibility for the ministry's success. It's natural to both want your church to believe they made the right choice and to put your stamp on the ministry. But trying to make a mark too soon without adequate information and buy-in may turn what seems like early wins into losses. Unless you have clearly defined reality (the next chapter) and are practicing listening and learning (chapter 2), acting too soon in big ways may send you down the wrong path. If you act too soon by focusing on tactics or move in multiple directions at once simply to create movement, you can confuse others about what's truly important. Should this happen, you may be saying yes to good ideas at the expense of the best ideas.

I recommend that new leaders prioritize spending time with key influencers just to listen. Again, recall the **PALM** acronym. "L" stands for listen and learn. Leaders who onboard well avoid busyness and prioritize relationships with key stakeholders and influencers to learn from them. Watkins notes this.

> ...*if you habitually find yourself too anxious or too busy to devote time to learning, you may suffer from the action imperative. It is a serious affliction, because often, being too busy to learn results is a death spiral. ... you can easily make poor early decisions that undermine your credibility, alienate potential supporters, and make people less likely to share important information with you. The result is that you make more bad decisions and enter a vicious cycle that can irreparably damage your credibility.*[80]

However, it is equally important to get tangible results and secure some early wins (see chapter 9 on building trust). Although you may be tempted to force change too quickly, it's important to bring change that will enhance your credibility as you address burning ministry issues. Your church will expect you to bring change, but be careful about pushing it until you know the culture (the next chapter), are convinced that your leaders are onboard, and you've created a clear change plan (chapter 3).

You'll want to show visible movement during your first six months without wrecking things or losing support. And you'll want to balance *being*

---

80   Watkins, *The First 90 Days*, p. 48.

with others with *doing* ministry tasks. In chapter 3 on change management, I suggested several brain-friendly change concepts to remember.

As Abraham Lincoln, America's sixteenth president, said in his inaugural address as the U.S. was sharply divided over slavery, "Nothing valuable can be lost by taking time."[81]

Pitfall # 6. Scaredy-Cat: Risk aversion

I excelled in science and math as a kid, and in college I earned an engineering degree. As a result, my education and personality incline me to analyze and gather lots of facts before I make decisions. Although good decision-making requires adequate data gathering, early in my ministry I tended to wait too long in order to gather more facts before making a decision. Sometimes I got sucked into analysis paralysis. I subconsciously thought that one more fact would guarantee that I would make the right choice. As a result, it appeared to some high-capacity leaders in my church that I was dragging my feet and not acting out of faith.

Minimizing risk and maximizing safety can become an unhealthy trait for leaders. J. Oswald Sanders, who authored the book *Spiritual Leadership,* quoted a Christian leader who noted, "The frontiers of the kingdom of God were never advanced by men and women of caution."[82] Great churches can't play it safe, huddle and cuddle, strive for safety and security, nor guarantee comfort and convenience. While not throwing caution to the wind, great leaders and churches must take bold steps of faith.

Golf provides a compelling visual metaphor for this unhealthy leadership quality. A golfer scores a birdie when he sinks the ball in one less stroke than par. He scores a bogie when he sinks it one stroke over par. Some leaders miss great opportunities (birdies) when they play it safe. They end up as *bogey* leaders.

---

81 "Inaugural Addresses of the Presidents of the United States: from George Washington 1789 to George Bush 1989," Text, accessed May 21, 2019, http://avalon.law.yale.edu/19th_century/lincoln1.asp.

82 J. Oswald Sanders, *Spiritual Leadership: Principles of Excellence for Every Believer,* New edition (Chicago, IL: Moody Publishers, 2007), Kindle e-book loc 2820.

Researchers at the Wharton School at the University of Pennsylvania analyzed over 2.5 million putts from the top twenty golfers on the PGA tour in 2007 and made a surprising discovery.[83] Prompted by fear of a bogey, these golfers often played it safe in tournaments. Their fear resulted in an average one-stroke loss per seventy-two-hole tournament, with a combined annual loss of $1.2 million in potential prize money. The agony of a bogey seemed to outweigh the thrill of a birdie.

This dynamic, called loss or risk aversion, occurs when fear of loss stifles our attempts at gain. As a result, that fear can result in missed opportunities because we lead (or golf) too conservatively. In fact, our brains seem to be wired this way. Two-thirds of the cells in the fight-flight structures of our brain (the amygdala) are wired to look for potential bad news (the negativity bias I referred to earlier). Personal experience confirms that we tend to more easily remember bad things than good. And we more quickly form bad impressions of others than good ones. Unfortunately, some leaders give in to this tendency too easily and make leadership decisions to avoid loss instead of achieving gain. So what can a leader do to minimize risk aversion? I suggest what I call the 3-C approach: counsel, certainty, and confidence.

Counsel: seek it. When you feel you're about to play it safe when faced with an important decision, seek counsel from wise people. You might choose your staff, your board, a close friend, or a coach. Often input from an objective person can give us needed insight to pull the trigger, or not. The writer of Proverbs encourages us to do this: *Plans go wrong for lack of advice; many advisers bring success* (Prov 15:22 NLT). One leader tasked with a major company turnaround said, "Get enough (facts) to feel comfortable, then make a decision and move on. People who sit around for too long analyze and reanalyze, and that's a pitfall if you're in a crisis."[84]

---

83   Strategic Management and North America, "Avoiding the Agony of a 'Bogey': Loss Aversion in Golf - and Business," accessed May 21, 2019, http://knowledge.wharton.upenn.edu/article/avoiding-the-agony-of-a-bogey-loss-aversion-in-golf-and-business/.

84   Neff and Citrin, *You're in Charge,* Kindle e-book loc. 3974.

Certainty: get it. Our brains love certainty.[85] We want to know what lies just around the corner. But often we have no control over the future. Every decision brings with it some uncertainty because we can't guarantee most outcomes. In response to uncertainty, the flight-fight part of our brain secretes chemicals that elicit fear, which can demotivate us. That's where faith must come in. Faith is confidence in the One who *is* most certain, God Himself. To overcome this fear prompted by the uncertainty of decision-making, we must place our confidence in the one thing we can be sure of, God's faithfulness. He'll give us that extra boost of certainty we need to make the right decision.

Courage: live it. Courage counters fear. It doesn't remove it. When fear rises before a decision, perhaps it's a sign that we're on the right track. Mark Twain said it well when he wrote, "Courage is resistance to fear, mastery of fear— not absence of fear." And as I wrote earlier, John Wayne, the venerable cowboy of cowboys, offers great advice when fear hinders taking a reasonable risk, "Courage is being scared to death—but saddling up anyway."

Finally, remember that risk aversion shows up in two ways: sticking with the familiar instead of the important and focusing on what you like to do instead of what you need to do.

Pitfall # 7. People Pleaser: Saying *Yes* to too many things

Bad stuff happens to leaders who say *yes* to too many things. You can lose control of your calendar. You can work too many hours. Your family can suffer. Stress can become toxic. And ultimately, your walk with Christ and your leadership can suffer.

Saying *yes* is easy and saying *no* is hard because when we say *no*, we almost always disappoint somebody else. And when we disappoint another, at least for a few moments, their disapproving comments or facial expressions can

---

85   David Rock, "Managing with the Brain in Mind," strategy+business, accessed May 21, 2019, http://www.strategy-business.com/article/09306?gko=5df7f.

make us feel rejected. Rejection hurts because social pain registers in our brain in the same place where physical pain registers.[86] Sensing another's disappointment in us feels bad. That's why we try to avoid it.

During your first six months, it's important to avoid adding unnecessary commitments to your already-full schedule. Remind yourself that you don't have to say *yes* to every invitation or new ministry idea, even though each request may initially appeal to you. Learn how to say *no* gracefully. This is perhaps one of the most important self-leadership skills to help you manage your margins early on. Here are five ways to develop that skill:

1. *Say no without using the word, "no."* In some settings, the word *no* itself can come across too harsh. Sometimes using other phrases like these can soften your response and yet still convey a *no*.

   My schedule simply won't permit it now. I don't have the bandwidth. Thanks for thinking about me though.

   I'd love to, but right now I can't. Can you ask me again next week (or whatever timeframe seems appropriate)?

   I'm sorry but it won't work now.

2. *Pause a few seconds before giving an answer to someone.* Because we don't want to disappoint people, we often default to a quick *Yes*. To avoid this, learn to pause a few seconds before responding to someone who asks you for a commitment. That short pause will buy you some time to frame your response, whether it is an appropriate *yes* or a *no*. Pausing can also give you time to consider what you'd have to give up were you to say *yes*.

3. *Delay your response when you honestly aren't sure how to respond.* Sometimes the ask may be valid, and you should take more time

---

86   Naomi I. Eisenberger, "Social Pain and the Brain: Controversies, Questions, and Where to Go from Here," *Annual Review of Psychology* 66 (January 3, 2015): 601–29, https://doi.org/10.1146/annurev-psych-010213-115146.

before deciding. In that case, tell the person that you can't give him a decision now but that you'd like to check your calendar and think more about it. If it does become a *no*, you will have created sufficient time to consider the pros and cons and then to frame a gracious *no*. If your boss or board asks you for something that will cause you to push other important projects aside, tactfully explain the situation and your willingness to say *yes* if they deem the project more important than the other projects. If they do, then graciously ask for their advice on how to re-prioritize your current commitments so that you can follow through on your *yes*.

4. *Ask them to email you with their request.* I've found that when people want me to make a decision on the spot, putting the onus back on them often results in a default *no*. So I will ask them to email me their request. Often, they never do, which becomes a default *no*. I developed this simple script that I've used in different ways when someone asked me to take on a commitment.

That really sounds interesting. Thanks for sharing it with me. As I begin here at WestPark, I want to make sure I am at my best for the church, which means I want to steward my time well and make sure that when I make a commitment, I can keep it. So in these first few months, I'm being careful about saying yes to many things that require my commitment until I figure out what I should focus on. So I can't say yes, but I'm not saying no either. If you would please email the details about this, I will consider it.

5. *Simply and kindly say, no, and if possible, explain why.* Sometimes you immediately know you should say *no*. In that case, a firm but gracious *no* is appropriate. It may feel awkward, but that uncomfortable emotion will quickly pass. However, if you say *yes* when you should have said *no*, the feelings of regret last much longer and take a much greater toll, notwithstanding the extra time to which you've now committed yourself.

I appreciate how author William Ury describes the value of saying *no*. "Like all good *No's*, ours were in a service to a higher *Yes*."[87] As pastors, we must keep in mind our higher *yesses*.

Saying *no* helps you set clear boundaries. Without them, you can create a vicious cycle. If you commit to more and more, others will demand more and more of you and will nibble away at your family and personal time. The result? You may become resentful and angry at the very people you are called to serve, thus impairing your leadership.

General Principles to Help Avoid These Pitfalls

Although I've shared several suggestions above, consider these general guidelines that can help you avoid these pitfalls:

- Weekly review the seven pitfalls to keep them on your radar. Remember, these are often subtle issues that aren't top of mind. In the first six months, make them top of mind. You can download the *Pitfalls Checklist* on the book freebies website.∞
- Have someone ask you about how you're dealing with these pitfalls. They could be a coach, a fellow pastor, a friend in your current or former church, or even your spouse. A simple email from them like, "Just checking in. Are you avoiding the pitfalls?" can be a great reminder.
- Humbly admit when you fall into one, and quickly climb out.
- And of course, pray that God's Spirit would give you the spiritual sensitivity to avoid them.

This question may help motivate you to avoid these pitfalls: How do I want to be remembered after my last six months in this ministry? Our answer makes us think about the Stephen Covey quote from his famous book, *The Seven Habits of Highly Effective People*, "Begin with the end in mind."

---

87   William Ury, *Getting to Yes with Yourself: And Other Worthy Opponents*, First Edition (New York, NY: HarperOne, 2015), p. 2.

As you reflect over these pitfalls, let the *end in mind* motivate you to avoid them.

In this chapter, we've looked at seven major pitfalls to avoid during your first six months, the second phase, "S," in the **SADDLE** process. In the next chapter, I'll unpack the third step, *Define Reality*, when we examine how you can begin to understand the culture of your new church, an onboarding essential.

———

Onboarding tips from an expert: Tim Stephens (www.leadingsmart.com), VP of Consulting, Vanderbloemen Search Group, former Executive Pastor, Granger Community Church, Granger, Indiana

- *The best thing a new ministry leader can do during the first six months:* Find out who the influencers are in the church. They might be folks who hold no positions and have little involvement. But who are the people that everyone looks to for approval of a new direction? Invest in those people. Don't try to remove their influence—instead, try to leverage their influence and discover what passions they have that line up with your vision.
- *The dumbest thing Tim has ever heard that a pastor did the first six months:* On his very first Sunday, the pastor announced he would be turning up the volume at all services in order to reach younger people. For the next several months, he spent all his time answering emails and trying to regain credibility with the seniors.

Pause and reflect question: In your prior ministries, which pitfall have you tended to fall into? What can you do to avoid falling into it again in your new role?

Next-step application: Share your pitfall tendency with a pastor friend and ask them to email you each month to ask what you're doing to avoid that pitfall.

CHAPTER 6

DEFINE REALITY

The first responsibility of a leader is to define reality.
— Max De Pree

⌐⌐

Chapter snapshot:

Start early
Avoid common pitfalls
Define reality
Develop a game plan
Lead your team
Establish trust

A new ministry leader must understand as much about the new setting as possible because you don't know what you don't know. In this chapter, I suggest five ways to define reality:

1. Take your church's pulse.
2. Decipher the unwritten code.
3. Discover wounds from the past.
4. Clarify the church's overall health stage.
5. Match strategy to situation.

I'll never forget the first advice I received during my first week in Canada. One of our elders had invited me to join him at a luncheon with local pastors and businesspeople. We had just moved, and I hadn't even spent a day in the office. I chatted with several people at the luncheon and asked what advice they'd give me as an American pastor new to Canada. I only remember what one pastor said. His first comment was foreboding. He said, "Lots of American pastors have come to Canada and failed miserably." I gulped and asked, "Why?" I needed to hear his answer. "They failed because they didn't practice collaborative leadership. They led with a command and control method."

In other words, he was saying that many American pastors used the Moses style of leadership (directional: this is what God says and we must do it) rather than the Barnabas style (influence: build trust and build relationships with other decision-makers). For the next several days, I mulled over his response and decided to heed it. His advice saved me much grief. That brief conversation motivated me to become a more collaborative leader, and it paid off. His perspective helped me refine my leadership style and guided me as I tried to define reality at my new church.

When you come into a new role, you'll tend to focus on tactics and strategies (rather than culture) since it's easier to make visible changes in those areas. Although defining reality includes understanding existing policies, procedures, tactics, etc., you must learn your ministry's culture. Every church and ministry have a particular ethos that defines who it is and what it does. Watkins offers a good working definition of culture, "a set of consistent patterns people follow for communicating, thinking, and acting, all grounded in their shared assumptions and values."[88]

In T. Scott Daniels' excellent book, *The First 100 Days*, he concludes that the angels John writes about in Revelation represent this ethos or culture that can be either good or bad. He writes, "The seven angels of the churches, to whom John writes, are neither disconnected spiritual beings

---

88   Watkins, *The First 90 Days*, p. 30.

nor merely a colorful way of describing nonexistent realities. Instead, the term 'angel' signifies the very real ethos or communal essence that either gives life to or works at destroying the fabric of the very community that gave birth to it."[89] So it behooves you to discover the "angel" in your new ministry.

Numbers 13:17-20 tells us how Moses sent twelve spies to scout out the promised land for forty days. He gave them specific instructions to help them define reality in several areas. Here's how he instructed the search party.

> When Moses sent them to explore Canaan, he said, "Go up through the Negev and on into the hill country. See what the land is like and whether the people who live there are strong or weak, few or many. What kind of land do they live in? Is it good or bad? What kind of towns do they live in? Are they unwalled or fortified? How is the soil? Is it fertile or poor? Are there trees on it or not? Do your best to bring back some of the fruit of the land." (It was the season for the first ripe grapes.) (NIV)

He wanted them to thoroughly analyze the people who lived there, the land they lived on, the towns they lived in, and the agricultural condition. They discovered that the land indeed *flowed with milk and honey.* Their analysis also revealed obstacles, giants in the land. The more Moses knew about the land, the better prepared he'd be to lead the people to settle there.

When you first arrive in your new ministry setting, you'll probably only see milk and honey as well. It's called the honeymoon stage. Yet the job of defining reality requires that you not only see opportunities but that you discover the issues and obstacles that could impede your progress. You can respond like the ten spies did with fear and hesitancy, or you can respond with courage and initiative as Joshua and Caleb did.

---

89   T. Scott Daniels, *The First 100 Days: A Pastor's Guide* (Beacon Hill Press, Kansas City, 2001), p. 40.

Avoid gathering information willy-nilly. Sometimes one person with a strong personality can convince you that their opinion represents reality. A structured learning process can help moderate those voices while amplifying the quieter ones you need to hear. This stage never ends. Even if you apply every suggestion I make below, you will never fully define reality. Culture never remains static and discerning it never ends. As I wrote in chapter 2, stay teachable by listening and learning.

Let's look, now, at the third letter in the **SADDLE** strategy, "D," for *Define Reality*, and the five ways to do that.

1. Take Your Church's Pulse

When you visit the doctor, their nurse/assistant will check at least three body readings: your temperature, your blood pressure, and your pulse. Those readings will quickly indicate if something is wrong. You'll want to take some early "ministry" readings as well when you begin your new role. Asking questions in different ways and of different people will give you those readings. I spend the bulk of this chapter on taking your church's pulse rather than on the other four ways because it is the core process by which we discern reality.

Earlier I suggested three sets of questions to ask in the early, mid, and late pre-hiring phase. Now that you've arrived, you'll want to develop and target new questions to different groups of people: stakeholders, key volunteers, fellow staff, and your board/boss. You may even want to reach out to the person whose shoes you filled. I would do this only with permission from the search team or your board/boss.

The Church's Overall Direction

Begin by clarifying the church's overall direction reflected in its stated mission, vision, and values/strategy statements. Here's the difference in the three: *We do this (the what: the mission) because of this (the why: our vision) by this (the how: our values/strategy)*. Unfortunately, such statements often become mere slogans etched on a plaque rather than beliefs and behaviors embraced by the church and leadership as a whole. Discern if that is the case. I learned that WestPark had spent many hours creating a mission statement even though only one elder could quote it when asked. I was careful, however, not to dismiss their prior work when I later led us in a new strategic planning process. So first discover what exists on paper and then dig deeper.

Will Mancini, church consultant and author of the seminal book, *Church Unique*, compares his mission/vision/values paradigm with a similar paradigm Patrick Lencioni (author and leadership consultant) suggests in his book *The Advantage*. This comparison can help you ask the right questions about mission/vision/values/strategy. [90]

- *Mission:* a clear statement of what your church is supposed to be doing:
  - Lencioni: Why do we exist?
  - Mancini: What do we do?

- *Values:* shared beliefs that guide the church's actions and reveal its strengths:
  - Lencioni: How do we behave?
  - Mancini: Why do we do what we do?

- *Strategy:* the overall process that shows how the church accomplishes its mission:
  - Lencioni: How will we succeed?
  - Mancini: How do we do what we do?

- *Success measures:* individual characteristics and attributes that indicate the church is accomplishing its mission:
  - Lencioni: What do we do?
  - Mancini: When are we successful?

---

90   Will Mancini, "How Patrick Lencioni's 6 Questions Relate to the Vision Frame's 5 Questions," *Will Mancini* (blog), August 10, 2012, https://www.willmancini.com/blog/how-patrick-lencionis-6-questions-relate-to-the-vision-frames-5-questions.

- *Vision*: language that illustrates and anticipates the better future God has in store for the church:
  - Lencioni: What is most important right now?
  - Mancini: Where are we going?

Use the above questions with key stakeholders, leaders, and staff to help clarify the church's culture in those categories. You'll also want to define reality in the areas below:

- *Finances*: What is the church's budget, current giving, and giving history?
- *Job descriptions*: What are the current written job descriptions for staff and volunteers in your area?
- *Policies and procedures*: Get a copy of the staff/office policy handbook if it exists.
- *Community*: Learn about the demographics of the community the church serves.
- *Systems*: What ministry systems exist?
- *Board/church minutes*: If the board and church keep minutes of its meetings, read those from the past year or two.

Staff and Key Volunteers

Next, try to define reality through your staff and key volunteers. Staff meetings and one-on-ones with your staff and volunteers will provide great insight into current reality. At the first staff meeting I attended, I simply observed like a fly on the wall. I wanted to sense the team dynamics the best I could while recognizing that everybody was probably putting on their best behavior for the "new boss." The interim lead pastor was still on-board at the time, and he led the meeting.

At the second meeting, I asked the then-current worship pastor who had been at the church for many years to lead the staff in an exercise. I asked them to complete five statements I had modified from some questions in Neff and Citrin's book, *You're in Charge—Now What?*[91] I explained that

---

91   Thomas J. Neff and James M. Citrin, *You're in Charge, Now What?: The 8 Point Plan*, Reprint edition (New York: Crown Business, 2007), Kindle e-book loc. 958).

their honest feedback would help me understand their expectations. I then left the room so they'd be free to respond. The discussion lasted about thirty minutes and I then re-joined them. Here are the statements with their responses:

Statement 1 – *We expect this from you:*
- Shepherd and lead/guide us, care for us, pray for us.
- Provide feedback, evaluation; tell us the truth, correct us when needed.
- Be consistent and show integrity.
- Provide ideas, challenge, leadership growth, and training.
- Give us biblical teaching.

Statement 2 – *You need to know this about us (including what we do well and where we need to improve):*
- We want to know how we can do better.
- We need clarity about our individual roles and each other's role.
- We need to communicate with each other and with the church better.
- We support each other.
- We work hard.
- We pray together weekly.
- We care about people.

Statement 3 – *We want to know this about you. And here are our concerns:*
- What is your vision?
- What are your priorities and values?
- What are your boundaries?
- When and how do we talk to you?
- Do you want replies to every email?
- How will we do staff retreats?

- What are your personal struggles?
- We need to know if we are supporting you.

Statement 4 – Here are the burning issues currently facing the church:

- Finances
- How we move forward
- Reaching the younger demographic
- Trust issues among the church and leadership
- Building unity among the different church groups

Statement 5 – Here are the major obstacles you will face:

- Personal agendas
- Resistance to change

In addition to this initial, one-time fact-gathering exercise, I wrote in chapter two that I initiated a short weekly report a few weeks in that allowed me to monitor the pulse of our staff. Each week, I asked the staff to email me their response to four questions. My assistant then compiled them into one document that I later forwarded to the staff and board, minus anything personal.

1. What went well last week?
2. What didn't go well?
3. What are the three most important tasks you must accomplish in the upcoming week? We call this the Big Three, which we also verbally share in our weekly staff meetings.
4. How can I pray for you/what do you need from me?

Key Stakeholders

Next, I got the pulse from key stakeholders. Who might qualify as stakeholders in your setting? They might include those above you in the org chart or in influence (board chair, session, lead pastor, boss, long-term key church/ministry leaders and members), those below you (staff and/or volunteers who report to you), community leaders, former staff, and other local pastors and ministry leaders. I tried to get a representative cross-section that included young and old, long-time members, and new attendees. During the first two months, I gathered a list of about twenty-five stakeholders and reached out to them for one-on-one conversations.

In each meeting, I asked these same six questions. Identical questions help balance out any extreme answers you may get, either overly optimistic or overly pessimistic. It's important not to be overly influenced by the first few people who give you their opinions. Patterns you'll want to identify will surface when you ask identical questions. Over time their answers will create an accurate composite picture of reality. Here are the questions:

1. Tell me about yourself.
2. What's going well in your ministry and/or the church?
3. What is not going so well (ministry and/or the church) that you would like to see improved or addressed?
4. What burning question would you like to ask me?
5. If you were in my shoes, what would you focus on?
6. How can I pray for you?

I also used these questions in informal conversations with staff during the week and with church members on Sundays. I practiced a management technique with our staff popular in the 1980s called Management by Walking Around.[92] It's simply showing up informally at the water cooler or at a staff member's office or in the lobby after church to listen and encourage. Coupling that practice with some of those questions will help you define reality.

Here's a composite picture I gleaned from the question, "What would you do if you were in my shoes?"

• Pray.
• Encourage and give hope.

---

92 "What Is Management by Walking around (MBWA)? Definition and Meaning," BusinessDictionary.com, accessed May 22, 2019, http://www.businessdictionary.com/definition/management-by-walking-around-MBWA.html.

- Build teams.
- Provide accountability. I later realized this meant that they wanted me to communicate progress to the church.
- Provide vision.
- Develop leaders and volunteers.

This information-gathering process helped me define reality from our staff and key stakeholders' perspectives. I've included these two sets of questions in a download called *Key Staff/ Volunteer/ Stakeholder Questions*.∞

Volunteer Leaders

An Appreciative Inquiry was another crucial tool that helped me define reality. Essentially, an Appreciative Inquiry (AI) is a multi-hour learning experience to gain insight into the church's strengths and positive experiences. In contrast to a problem-solving scenario, AI "advocates collective inquiry into the best of what is in order to imagine what could be, followed by collective design of a desired future state that is compelling and, thus, does not require the use of incentives, coercion, or persuasion for planned change to occur.[93] It's discovering the best of *what is* through a collaborative process.

I convened an AI gathering of sixty key leaders within sixty days of my coming. In three hours one Sunday afternoon, I learned crucial insights about WestPark's past and the dreams these leaders held for the future. I've included an AI guide in the download section of the website. It's called *Appreciative Inquiry*.∞

SWOT is another valuable tool developed by the Stanford Research Institute in the 1960s. This tool helps leaders analyze internal strengths and weaknesses (the "S" and the "W") simultaneously as you examine external opportunities and threats (the "O" and the "T"). You can find these tools online, and I've included as a download the SWOT I created as an example (*SWOT Analysis Example*).∞

---

93   *Appreciative Inquiry,* http://www.gervasebushe.ca/appinq.htm, accessed May 22, 2019.

- As I listened a lot and used these tools and questions, the following issues surfaced. Had I not structured my learning process to define reality, I could have missed many of these.
- Lack of unity. One person shared that although the church shared a building, a budget, and a staff, it felt like we were still three distinct groups (Chinese congregation, the younger English speakers, and the seniors).
- The seniors had felt marginalized by some of the prior leaders. A generation gap was evident.
- A lack of trust existed between the church and the elders and between the elders and the staff.
- Communication to the church had suffered during the prior leadership transition.
- No intentional plan to build leaders existed.
- The church lacked fundamental systems for communications, HR, assimilation, worship service planning, and stewardship.
- For years, leaders had tolerated destructive relational patterns in some long-timers (i.e., a person's ongoing gruffness with others was excused as, "That's just Joe or Susie (not real names).")
- The church lacked a common vision.
- Small relational deposits mattered (like when I phoned an older man to ask how his niece was doing after her brain surgery).

As you take the pulse of your new ministry, keep a journal. I kept one and it helped me combine seemingly disparate thoughts and experiences into common themes. During my first year, I wrote almost 10,000 words in my journal, equivalent to two to three book chapters. Here's one particularly candid entry, which helped me learn:

Well, I've met with several people and I'm getting an earful. It's like a ball of twine with different sizes and lengths. The twine is a mass of angst, anger, emotion, disappointment with the church, and pent up frustration. As I mentally pull out each string, it represents each person's gripe, solution, what they want, their personal agenda. And it seems that everybody has their own personal agenda. The strings are going every which-a-way, and when that happens, there is no synergy and alignment in a church. As I've heard people's pet peeves and personal agendas, it's been discouraging to see this much energy and emotion around their issues. It's disappointing that I didn't get the true picture in the candidating process. Too much happy talk that everything was great.

This entry did not reflect the majority of my early experiences, but it captures my heart at that moment. Most of my experiences and journal entries were positive. Two positives about the past often surfaced in conversations. One was a day camp the church held on the church property before the building was built. Years prior, almost six hundred kids attended these camps. Another positive experience was something called the Annex. After the current church facility was built, the gym was opened every Friday night for neighborhood teens. It lasted about a year, and over one hundred teens came each week. These two recurring positives helped me see that the church wanted to reach kids and students. As you take the pulse of your church, note common stories people repeat. They will provide key clues to the culture.

In summary, you can take the pulse in several ways:
- Mission/vision/values/strategy: Discern the church's stated or implied direction.
- Staff/volunteers: Use the five statements exercise the first month.
- Staff: Ask staff/key volunteers to complete the four questions each week.
- Stakeholders: Use the six questions in both formal and informal conversations.
- Volunteer leaders: Hold an Appreciative Inquiry.
- Strengths/weaknesses: Do a SWOT analysis.

2. Decipher Its Unwritten Code

Early on, you'll quickly discern key issues about your new church. However, every church has an unwritten code, a *"shadow organization—*the informal set of processes and alliances that exist in the shadow of the formal structure and strongly influence how work actually gets done."[94]

Some might call this unwritten code or culture, church politics. Ronald Heifetz, author and business expert, calls discerning the unspoken as, "listening to the song beneath the words."[95] You must become a cultural archeologist and dig beneath the obvious to decipher the unwritten code as you search for unspoken expectations and realities. Before you design strategy or bring significant change, do your best to understand your ministry's culture. The statement, *Culture eats strategy for breakfast,* is often attributed to Peter Drucker, considered the father of modern management. I gave a simple definition of culture earlier, but these definitions further unpack the concept.

- Culture is "the language we live in, the artifacts that we make use of, the rituals we engage in, our approach to ethics, the institutions we are a part of, and the narratives we inhabit [that] have the power to shape our lives profoundly."[96]
- Culture is the "group norms of behavior and the underlying shared values that help keep those norms in place."[97]
- Culture acts like the body's DNA that, by default, replicates qualities of itself every time a cell is formed. In your church,

---

94 Watkins, *The First 90 Days,* p. 54.

95 Ronald A. Heifetz, Marty Linsky, and Alexander Grashow, *The Practice of Adaptive Leadership: Tools and Tactics for Changing Your Organization and the World,* 1 edition (Boston, Mass: Harvard Business Press, 2009), Kindle e-book loc. 4710.

96 J. R. Woodward and Alan Hirsch, *Creating a Missional Culture: Equipping the Church for the Sake of the World* (Downers Grove, IL: IVP Books, 2012), p. 20.

97 Kotter International, "The Key to Changing Organizational Culture," Forbes, accessed May 22,2019, http://www.forbes.com/sites/johnkotter/2012/09/27/the-key-to-changing-organizational-culture/.

culture replicates ways of doing things, whether by default or design. It just happens (source unknown).

You will run into significant roadblocks unless you develop a process to decipher the culture's unwritten code. One management expert succinctly wrote, "After working on strategy for twenty years, I can say this: culture will trump strategy, every time. The best strategic idea means nothing in isolation. If the strategy conflicts with how a group of people already believe, behave, or make decisions, it will fail. Conversely, a culturally robust team can turn a so-so strategy into a winner."[98]

You probably received documents like the church's bylaws and policies when you candidated. While they reveal a lot, they'll probably only loosely match reality. Most of the real rules aren't written down. As you develop your cultural archeologist skills, you'll learn to read between the lines by observing "how things really work around here." Remember, activities that give quick tangible results will tempt you. Resist that temptation. Instead, focus your effort on becoming a better cultural archeologist. As Citrin and Neff write, "A failure to assess the culture and the readiness for change among different interest groups can be lethal."[99]

I've listed below nine areas to consider as you try to decipher the church's unwritten code, along with questions to ask about those areas.

1. Meetings... How are meetings run?

I discovered that the staff seldom used an agenda. They just showed up and started talking. I also noticed that our elders strictly followed Robert's Rules of Order. And the church's bylaws were over thirty pages long. I came to realize that, for decades, accountants had greatly influenced the church. Since accountants are sticklers for details and exactness, they had influenced how elders' meetings were run and why the bylaws were so long.

---

98   Nilofer Merchant, "Culture Trumps Strategy, Every Time," *Harvard Business Review*, March 22, 2011, https://hbr.org/2011/03/culture-trumps-strategy-every.

99   Neff and Citrin, *You're in Charge, Now What?*, Kindle e-book locs. 2373.

I also learned that because the church had faced some difficult times that took significant discussion at the board level, some meetings had lasted four to five hours.

2. Decisions... How are they made?

It's important to understand the board and congregation's default decision-making style. If they expect one style and you use another, conflict may result. Onboarding experts Bradt, Check, and Pedraza suggest these five general decision-making styles.[100]

- I decide on my own.
- I decide with input from you.
- You and I decide together.
- You decide with my input.
- You decide on your own.

I mentioned earlier the advice a pastor gave me about the Canadian Church's preference for collaborative versus command and control leadership. I also discovered that our board made decisions collaboratively. Although I'm an elder, I have no vote on the board. My vote is my influence, so our style was "you decide with my input."

3. Success... How do the leaders and the church measure success? Is it the standard budgets, buildings, and bums (the Canadian word for our posterior) in the pews? Or are there other significant measures such as volunteers, external ministry, new visitors, and small group involvement?

4. Strategic direction... How did the current strategic direction get defined? Was it a thorough process, well-defined and embraced by the church? Or was it simply a process that was put into a notebook and placed on a shelf or a motto simply hung on a wall?

---

100   George B. Bradt, Jayme A. Check, and Jorge E. Pedraza, *The New Leader's 100-Day Action Plan: How to Take Charge, Build Your Team, and Get Immediate Results*, 3 edition (Hoboken, N.J: Wiley, 2011), Kindle e-book loc. 2790.

5. Influencers... Who are the shadow influencers?

I asked our board who the key stakeholders were. They gave me a list of those they called the 'wise ones.' I met with most of them in my one-on-one interviews. You may want to map out those influencers and discern if they tend to be supporters, opponents, indifferent, early or late adopters, or persuadable. Such insight might help you know how best to influence them. Earlier I wrote that Aristotle suggested that three domains affect how we influence others. It's worth repeating the three: Logos, persuasion through reasoning, data, and logic; Pathos, persuasion by appealing to emotions; and Ethos, persuasion through the force of character or personality of the speaker or writer. Keep these in mind as you seek to persuade your shadow influencers to embrace your change initiatives.

6. Conflict... How do people handle conflict? How have the staff, the board, and the people in general handled a recent conflict?

I soon realized that conflict resolution was not a strength of the church. I also believe that because British culture still influences Canadian culture, Canadians tend to avoid conflict rather than deal with it (at least not as outwardly as Americans might). I dealt with this in three ways. In my first series, the book of Nehemiah, I delivered two messages on conflict. Second, at our second leadership community meeting (a quarterly gathering of all our leaders and volunteers), the speaker spoke on courageous conversations, a way to handle conflict. Finally, seven months into my first year, I delivered a three-part sermon series on conflict resolution. On the third week, I handed out a business card printed with simple biblical steps to resolving conflict.

7. Communication... What is the preferred communication style? Is it formal or informal? What is the preferred frequency? How active is the grapevine?

8. Legacy... How did the employee you replaced operate? What were his or her strengths and weaknesses and leadership style?

9. Change... How have change initiatives gone in the past?

One of the downloads includes a list called, *Culture Discernment Questions.*∞

3. Discover Wounds from the Past

Most churches have faced painful experiences from the past with wounds that may linger. It's important to know how these might still affect the church's culture, without getting into unnecessary detail. I learned that over twenty-five years earlier, a church member had committed a heinous crime against his wife and was imprisoned as a result. Although the issue was long past, I was surprised to hear a Canadian border officer ask me about it when he saw on my passport that I pastored WestPark. In another incident many years prior, a pastor had left under difficult circumstances. Although no moral issues were involved, the leadership did not feel it was wise to share all the details with the church. As a result, people made up their own stories, which diminished their trust in the leadership.

I addressed these past wounds in two ways. First, I hired an expert who helps churches deal with such wounds. We gathered all current and former board members for a retreat, and he led us through a discussion and prayer process for healing. Second, we held an all-church solemn assembly, a church service patterned after biblical examples when God's people publicly repented. In preparation for our elder retreat, we called the church together for an evening of personal reflection and repentance. We read Scripture, allowed time for personal and private repentance, and sang hymns. Then, without using names and minimizing specific details, each elder stood and publicly read portions of a list of thirty-two attitudes that we felt needed public repentance. This was very powerful, and I believe it helped us move forward from some of the painful past. You can search the web for "solemn assembly" and find many resources to guide you should you feel a solemn assembly is warranted.

These questions might help you discover lingering wounds:
- What significant traumas or crises have marked your church's history?

- How has your church responded to them?
- What problems seem to recur in your church?
- Does your church have any deep, dark secrets?
- Did the church begin from a split? If so, what caused the split?
- Do staff generally stay only a short time? Is that a pattern?
- How have pastoral departures been handled? How do people talk about the church's prior pastors?
- Is there an ongoing pattern of firing staff or staff leaving under duress?
- Have any recurring sins persisted in staff or key leaders (sexual immorality, financial malfeasance, gossip, etc.)?

4. Clarify the Church's Overall Health Stage

Your church's health stage will determine how you'll develop your initial strategy because each stage demands a different plan. Unless you're planting a church, your new church will fall into one of the broad categories below, although you may notice some overlap. Below each stage, I've listed the qualities of a church in that stage.

Exceptional Stage
- Numerically growing
- Good financial health
- A sense of excitement about the future
- Unity at the board and staff level
- Immediate changes probably not needed
- A vision and ministry strategy that is clear and understood by the majority of the people
- General strategy: Build upon successes, preserve vitality, help the church avoid relying on strategies that brought past success, tweak things, and take the ministry to the next level.

Flat stage
- Little numerical growth
- Muddy or non-existent vision for the future
- Some dissension
- General strategy: Convince the people that change is necessary, create a sense of urgency, restructure leadership as needed, recognize and build upon current strengths, and bring change at a healthy pace.

On life-support stage (a church that probably needs resurrecting)
- Decline in growth and finances
- Hopelessness, discouragement, and fear
- Potentially significant dissension, or perhaps little dissention because the gloomy future may unite the people to do something dramatic to keep the church from dying
- General strategy: Invigorate morale, give hope, provide vision, make difficult choices, and act quickly, boldly, and decisively.

Non-existent/startup stage: In this category, you may be starting a new ministry in a church or starting a new church. You'll have much greater free reign in this setting and little or no prior baggage.

5. Match Strategy to Situation

By the time you arrive in your new setting, you probably have some idea what you'd like to accomplish and what your board or boss expects from you. But like the famous explorers Lewis and Clark, who thought they'd find a navigable waterway that traversed the eastern US to the west, they really didn't know what lay beyond the horizon. Ultimately, they discovered that no waterway existed, and they had to adjust their expectations.

You, too, will probably have to adjust your expectations somewhat as you define reality. But as reality becomes more clear, you'll know what you need to change and you'll feel more confident as you lead. As you progressively discern reality, you can wisely match your strategy to the current situation. In the next chapter, *Develop a Game Plan*, you'll learn how to create your strategy for the first six months. Watkins calls this a learning agenda.

In this chapter, you've begun to define reality, which will help you gain the insight you need to make good decisions. This process will also help you steward your time well so that you can say *yes* to the right things and help you focus your energies in the right direction.

So let's begin to put some meat on the bones in the next chapter as we look at creating your action plans for your first six months, the second "D" in the **SADDLE** process.

––––––

Onboarding tips from an expert: Dan Reiland, Executive Pastor, 12Stone Church, Lawrenceville, Georgia (www.danreiland.com)

- *The best thing a new pastoral ministry leader can do during the first six months:* Learn the culture. Nothing will eat your lunch faster than being clueless about the culture. Make your relational connections from a heart level. People know when you love them and when you use them. Don't initiate any change just to make things different. Initiate change to make things better.

- *The dumbest thing Dan has ever heard that a pastor did the first six months:* Removed the pulpit that was built by the grandfather of the pastor that founded the church just to put in a smaller, cooler pulpit.

Pause and reflect question: Of the five ways I suggest to define reality, which one seems most daunting? Why?

Next-step application: As you think about the one that seems most daunting, what can you do to create more certainty about that concern? Remember, the brain dislikes uncertainty, so if you can create a specific action plan to address that area—thus increasing certainty—it won't seem as emotionally draining to you or others.

CHAPTER 7

DEVELOP A GAME PLAN

You shouldn't expect to walk into a new leadership job with an established strategic plan. Rather, you should walk in prepared to lead a strategic process.[101]
—Thomas Neff and James Citrin

∿

Chapter snapshot:

Start early
Avoid common pitfalls
Define reality
Develop a six-month Game Plan
Lead your team
Establish trust

A six-month game plan forms an essential building block for effective onboarding. It's a thoughtfully designed and flexible template that guides your leadership for the first six months in a new ministry role. These four essentials comprise a good game plan.

---

101   Neff and Citrin, *You're in Charge,* Kindle e-book loc. 286.

> 1. Begin with the end in mind.
> 2. Craft the story you want others to believe about you.
> 3. Secure and celebrate early wins.
> 4. Write down your plan.

In one of the most famous father-in-law, son-in-law encounters, Moses was proudly showing Jethro, his father-in-law, how God had used him to lead the children of Israel out of Egyptian bondage. Jethro expressed his joy in how the Lord was working through Moses. Yet the next day when Jethro observed Moses' day-to-day leadership, (being the go-to guy for every issue the people faced), he spoke these words to Moses. *"What you are doing is not good. You and these people who come to you will only wear yourselves out. The work is too heavy for you; you cannot handle it alone. Listen now to me and I will give you some advice, and may God be with you* (Exod 18:17-19 NIV).

Jethro wisely observed that if Moses continued leading as he did, ultimately, he would burn out. He then gave Moses wise counsel to change his leadership style. He told Moses to stop doing everything, take the difficult cases, and delegate the rest. Jethro suggested a new game plan and Moses heeded it.

As you begin your new ministry, it's important that you, too, craft a good six-month game plan. In this chapter we'll examine the fourth letter in the **SADDLE** strategy, "D," for *Develop a Six-Month Game Plan*, a specific, yet flexible guide that describes what you hope to accomplish in your first six months. It's less like a strategic *plan* and more like a strategic *process* because during the first six months, you don't know enough to create a detailed action plan, an in-depth strategy, or a vision statement. A good game plan, however, will help you shape things before they shape you and offers these benefits.

- It will help you answer five questions in people's minds.
  - Who am I?
  - Where do I come from?

- Why am I here?
- What do I plan to accomplish?
- How do I hope to do it?[102]

- It will keep you on track and help you pace yourself. You'll be tempted to focus on minutia and activities that don't necessarily contribute to your overall success. A clear game plan, however, will help keep your focus on what's most important and keep first things first. You can't do everything, and a game plan can help you know when to say *yes* and when to say *no.*

- It will give you a clear measure against which to evaluate progress for you, the church, and your leadership. People want to see progress, yet many church leaders fail to set clear benchmarks against which to evaluate such progress. A game plan will provide clear markers to help you gauge progress and forward momentum.

- It will help you leverage your gifts, experience, and calling. The church hired you because they saw in you the qualities needed for the new role. They rightly expect you to use your gifts to maximize Kingdom impact.

- It will help you know what you need to know to effectively communicate. Often, ministry staff and volunteers expect that their ministry should be prioritized when programs get communicated, whether during Sunday announcements, via printed material, or electronically. A clear game plan will help you decide what must take priority in the church's communication plan.

---

102   Ibid, loc. 835.

1. Begin with the End in Mind.

Several years ago, the late Stephen Covey popularized the concept, "Begin with the end in mind." This principle should guide you as you start to create your game plan. Imagine yourself six months out from your first day. How would you complete these statements? You can download a *Begin with the End in Mind* template at the book website to help you complete these statements.∞

At the end of six months, I want...

...people to believe this story about me:

...to have secured these wins/successes:

...to have used these venues to communicate my game plan:

...to have held conversations with these key people:

...to have communicated progress to the church/ministry in these ways:

Think about how you'd answer each of these. Below, I've explained them in more detail and given some examples. As ideas come to mind, jot them down on the template and then transfer key dates related to goals and action plans to your calendar. You'll first determine the *what* and then you'll schedule the *when*.

Begin forming your plan even before your first day in the office. In addition to the six months I suggest for your onboarding plan, factor in the "minus" weeks what you should do during the few weeks prior to day one. Before I began at WestPark, I asked the staff and elders to complete individual personality inventories, and I also asked them to answer the six stakeholder questions I wrote about in the prior chapter. I repeat them here:

1. What can you tell me about yourself?
2. What's going well in your ministry and/or the church?
3. What is not going so well (ministry and/or the church) that you would like to see improved or addressed?
4. What burning question would you like to ask me?
5. If you were in my shoes, what would you focus on?
6. How can I pray for you?

This information, plus answers to questions I posed during the candidating phase, helped me begin to fashion my game plan as I sensed what I felt God wanted me to address the first six months.

It's helpful to revisit the reason for a six-month window versus the traditional ninety/one-hundred-day window a new leader in business or the political arena might adopt. In the introductory chapter, I suggested a six-month window because churches tend to move slower than businesses. Unless the ship is sinking and you must quickly make drastic changes, six months is probably the ideal window. That time frame allows you to cover two ministry seasons. And based on business research, which I believe applies to ministry, "It takes a new mid-level manager at least six months to reach the break-even point even in an organization where they are a good fit and have a good chance of success."[103] Although you may find that four months or eight months works best for you, six months is probably the sweet spot.

2. Craft the Story You Want Others to Believe about You.

The adage "you don't have a second chance to make a good first impression" is grounded in science. One study discovered that people determine their impressions of others in 1/10 of a second.[104] Other studies show that within a few seconds of meeting someone, people form impressions about his or her trustworthiness, leadership ability, intelligence, and conscientiousness.[105] Don't become paranoid about these facts, though.

---

103 Ray Williams, "Onboarding Increases Probability of Leaders' Success," *Financial Post* (blog), accessed May 22, 2019, http://business.financialpost.com/executive/careers/onboarding-increases-probability-of-leaders-success.

104 Eric Wargo, "How Many Seconds to a First Impression? - Association for Psychological Science," accessed November 6, 2015, http://www.psychologicalscience.org/index.php/publications/observer/2006/july-06/how-many-seconds-to-a-first-impression.html.

105 Shana Lebowitz, "Science Says People Decide These 13 Things within Seconds of Meeting You," November 18, 2015, https://www.thejournal.ie/personalty-meeting-2461308-Nov2015/, accessed May 22, 2019.

Well-known church consultant Kennon Callahan is more realistic when he says that our first *days* will shape our first three weeks.[106] So as you initially relate to others, realize that people will quickly form their impressions about you.

Your first day in the office, the first time you teach, the first meeting with your key volunteers, and the first staff meeting you attend or lead are all crucial *firsts* to carefully consider. Because the brain tends to remember what was first and last, called the *primacy* and *recency effect*, respectively, give considerable thought to what you say and do during those first experiences.

People naturally create stories about other people, and your leaders, volunteers, staff, and people in your church are no different. Give them reasons to make up a good story about you. Be intentional about guiding the narrative that people will create about you. You want the grapevine to work in your favor.

I prayerfully developed the following list of qualities that I believed God wanted me to model that I, in turn, hoped the church would believe about me. And I planned specific tasks to help me portray that story. I didn't do this selfishly to manipulate people. Rather, I felt that they needed to see these qualities in me so I could gain their trust and thus lead the church well, especially during those first six months.

Below I've listed those qualities and included a few steps I included in my game to support them.

After six months, I hope the people at WestPark will form this story about me in their minds and hearts:

That my teaching is informative, inspiring, and transformative.

- I blocked out significant hours each week to prepare strong sermons, and I seldom let anything intrude into those hours.
- I preached through the book of Nehemiah, which naturally allowed me to broach problem areas the church faced.

---

106 Kennon L. Callahan, *A New Beginning for Pastors and Congregations: Building an Excellent Match Upon Your Shared Strengths*, 1st edition (San Francisco: Jossey-Bass, 1999), p 6.

- I began each sermon with a personal anecdote about myself or my family (with their permission of course).

That I really listen.

- I scheduled over twenty-five one-on-one interviews with key people.
- I scheduled an Appreciative Inquiry with sixty leaders within two months (see the prior chapter).
- I often reminded people during Sunday messages that one of my biggest goals was to listen and learn.

That I'm an encourager.

- I tried to remember the personal issues people faced, and when I saw them, I would ask them how they were doing.
- Almost every week, I thanked the church during the offering time for their faithful financial support.

That I'm being proactive about building trust.

- I had our staff read, study, and dialogue about how to build trust. (I devote the entire next chapter to that subject.)
- I delivered a message on trust.
- I scheduled time for the elder board to discuss trust.

That I'm knowable and approachable.

- I moved the location where I preached from the stage to a small platform on the floor. While on stage, I stood about three feet above everyone else, which created an artificial barrier. This move created a more intimate setting.
- I began my "Where's Waldo" blurb in the weekly bulletin, where I summarized a few personal highlights from the prior week.
- Before each service, I circulated among the people to greet them and made myself available at the welcome center each week after each service.

- During the first few weeks, I attended several senior's events as well as events held by other ministries in our church.

This intentional plan to create my story worked. When I met with one of the "wise ones" I asked him what he would suggest I do. He said to do what I was currently doing, listen. He had heard through the grapevine that I listened well and that I was not trying to radically change things in the church, which some feared might happen.

In addition to intentional behaviors you will *do* to help the people fashion their story about you, you'll also want to *avoid* some behaviors such as these:

- Don't be late for meetings.
- Don't tell any but the mildest jokes.
- Avoid inappropriate dress (find out what the dress code is before day one).
- Don't criticize or speak ill of your prior ministry or boss.
- Don't talk too much about yourself.

As you seek to fashion the church's growing narrative about you, use every interaction in a non-manipulative way as an opportunity to plant seeds about your story.

3. Secure and Celebrate Early Wins.

In chapter 5, you'll recall that one of the pitfalls to avoid is "overemphasis on quick results." "Secure early wins" may seem contradictory, but here's the difference. It's a pitfall when you seek a win just to justify your hiring or you seek a win without enough information. It's beneficial, though, when those wins are *low-hanging fruit* that most people would view as a win, wins that won't cause much controversy from change, or leave some people sensing they lost something.

Your early wins should also advance the church's long-term goals and objectives. One key study of business executives in transition discovered that leaders most successfully make changes in successive waves to allow their organizations to adjust before making new changes. Each wave includes distinct phases: learn, build support, implement, and observe the results.[107]

Early wins help build your credibility and the story others are creating about you. And people will seek to confirm their story. It's called the confirmation bias. Your early wins will either confirm their story about you or help them create a new one. Early ministry wins that you communicate well build the trust you will need to later bring change that may not be as easy as the low-hanging fruit.

Ask yourself what changes could bring such early wins without causing much consternation. What would most people view as a common win? What win could be visible to most people or to the influencers?

Consider these ideas on how to select an early win.

- Focus on the ones that would matter most to the church's long-term health and vision, not just the ones that appeal to you or ones that seem easiest to effect.
- Don't try to accomplish too many wins. Pick a few achievable ones. It's better to underpromise and overperform.
- Choose wins that would matter to your board or boss.
- Pick wins that you can deliver, not unrealistic ones.
- Pick wins that would not have been accomplished had you not come.
- Pick them within the first month or two.
- Ideally, pick ones your team can contribute to. You want your team to view the win as their win rather than your win.
- Invest adequate energy, time, focus, and resources into your wins. Since they'll probably take more resources than you think, plan accordingly.

As an example, I've listed below seven key early wins I set out to achieve as well as some action plans related to each. You'll notice that I didn't include a numerical attendance goal that pastors usually set. Although

---

107 Watkins, *The First 90 Days,* pp. 116-118.

important, I waited to set numerical goals until a year later because I didn't want people to think that ministry was all about numbers.

Early Wins I Sought to Achieve

1. *Create listening and learning* anchors (leadership assessments of staff and elders, one-on-one meetings with key stakeholders, weekly email updates from staff, appreciative inquiry with sixty leaders within two months).

2. *Enhance communication* (weekly email updates to elders about my progress, "Where's Waldo" bulletin blurb, meeting with all volunteers to give a progress report 60 days in, provide a written progress report to the church 60, 90, and 180 days in).

3. *Improve giving* (have an end-of-year offering to pull us out of the financial hole, develop a strategic stewardship plan, weekly put a face on giving by telling a story or showing a picture before the offering time to illustrate where the church's money goes).

4. *Develop leaders* (carry out a staff and elder retreat, begin quarterly leadership gatherings for vision casting, training, and reporting progress).

5. *Build trust* (staff and elders study trust, deliver a message on trust, overcommunicate to people so they know what's happening).

6. *Begin the healing process* (gather leaders to pray through hurts of the past, call the church to a solemn assembly).

7. *Other* (preach on Nehemiah to naturally broach some crucial church issues, such as vision, conflict resolution, spiritual renewal, unity, and leadership development; find an interim worship leader).

In my first few months, I also created a general theme (sometimes called a Rally Cry or a Burning Imperative), *Unified yet Unique*. With the word *unique*, I wanted to capitalize on our diverse congregation (two separate services in different languages and our multi-generational demographic). I also wanted to subtly deal with a general lack of trust and some disunity by using the word *unified*. This theme also served as a pseudo mission statement placeholder until I began a re-visioning process two years later.

We celebrated our wins in several ways. I always included praise reports at our twice-monthly elder retreats. We began each staff meeting with the question, "What's going good?" Our staff would then share encouraging stories from our ministry. I'd often weave into my Sunday sermon praise or a story that illustrated God's work at the church. I arranged seating at our quarterly Leadership Communities around tables to foster community. I'd start those meetings by asking each person at their table to share what they were most excited about in their ministry at WestPark. I'd then ask one person from each table to stand and share a highlight they just learned with the entire group. This always created a celebratory atmosphere. Such wins can build your credibility and energize your people.

One caution, though. Don't equate an *early* win with a *big* win. Sometimes progress seen in small ways can best build the credibility and trust you need. You don't necessarily need huge wins early on. As one author noted, early wins are "the blasting caps, not the dynamite. They are the opening singles, not the grand slam home run."[108]

4. Write Down Your Plan.

It's extremely important that you write down your game plan. For an example of how a game plan might look, you can download a copy of the *Six-Month Game Plan Example* I shared with the elders within thirty days of arriving.∞ You can remove the detail from the download and create a template to help you design your own Six-Month Game Plan.

Don't wait until each day to decide what's important. Let your six-month game plan help you decide. A written plan provides personal accountability and accountability to your boss or board.

Each week I carved out three to four hours for strategic planning (and still do). I began my planning time with prayer. Then I reviewed and

---

108 Bradt, Check, and Pedraza, *The New Leader's 100-Day Action Plan,* Kindle ebook loc 4359.

modified my plan as needed. I would take specific tasks and put them in a calendar to remind me when they were due. And each week I also reviewed my calendar several weeks out to remind me about pending tasks. It's important to track and monitor your progress, and you can't unless you've written down your game plan. In chapter 10, I explain a twenty-six-week guide to help keep you on track the first six months. You may not allocate three to four hours each week as I do, but you probably need a minimum of two hours.

I've refined this weekly strategic planning to a system that serves me well. You might want to try it. Here's what I do during those three to four hours. On Sunday afternoons after church, I go to a nearby McDonalds to plan (free Wi-fi and free drink refills). I sit in the far corner, away from all distractions. These four hours have become some of the most profitable hours of my week. I follow this planning hierarchy.

- I re-read my *True North Values* (chapter 4) as well as my *Personal and Ministry Mission Statement* (both available as downloads).∞
- I review my written six-month game plan.
- I review a tool called the *Dashboard*,∞ where in one place I can see our mission, values, and major objectives.
- I adjust and tweak the plan by looking at thirty-day, three-month, and six-month objectives.
- I review my previous week and record what went well, what didn't go well, and what I learned.
- I review the upcoming four weeks and schedule times for projects that require extra planning time.
- I review an ongoing list of projects I keep in a software program called *Nozbe*. By reviewing these I create new action plans and schedule time to address projects that need prioritizing.
- I review the contents within what I call my *Red File*, a group of folders where I keep paper information about ongoing projects. This review prompts me to act upon some of the projects.

I encourage you to find a system for planning that works for you. Don't approach ministry with a, "Hmmm, I wonder what I will do today." Let your six-month game plan guide your actions.

In chapter 2, I explained that the "A" in the **PALM** acronym was *Avidly Over Communicate*. I described general communication principles and explained how and to whom I communicated during those early days. Your six-month game plan should also include specific people and groups you want to talk to and dates for those communications. Don't expect to effectively communicate if you rely on chance, your memory, or some serendipitous process. Be intentional. You might also want to review the first part of chapter 2 as you create your six-month game plan to make sure it includes a strong communication component.

Ideally, you can limit your game plan to a couple of pages. For some specific projects, you may need to create sub-documents with more detail, like my *Red File*, for example. I also found it useful to keep an ongoing journal where each day I briefly revisited the **PALM** and **SADDLE** strategies to record my progress, at least in the first six months. Then, during my weekly in-depth strategic review on Sundays, I would note trends, areas to which I needed to attend, and action plans for the upcoming week. Also, avoid two extremes. Don't get bogged down by making this process too detailed. At the same time, don't keep it so simple that it's useless.

A Few Final Thoughts

Create your office space for maximum efficiency. Do you prefer whiteboards or flip charts for brainstorming? Do you need to rearrange your office? Should you do your heavy thinking inside or outside the office? My office included a cubby hole with a small desk, which is out of sight of the hallway window. That has become my main workspace rather than a large desk that sits in my main office area.

View your six-month game plan as a living document. As you progressively discern reality, you'll need to tweak and modify it. It will never be perfect, so don't strive to make it so. Prioritize a weekly strategic review to make necessary changes.

In this chapter, I've unpacked how to create your six-month game plan. In the next chapter, I'll explain the "L" in the **SADDLE** process, *Lead Your Team.*

———

Onboarding tips from an expert: Kevin Stone, Founder of ExecutivePastoronline.com and Executive Pastor at Christ's Church of the Valley (CCVLive.com)

- *The best thing a new pastoral ministry leader can do during the first six months:* One thing I always recommend to people starting in a new role/new organization is to take an "eyes and ears open, mouth shut" approach. By this I mean, don't be too quick to make suggestions and try to solve problems. There are lots of reasons things are the way they are. You need time to learn the culture, history, industry (or ministry), etc. before you start making suggestions.

- *The dumbest thing Kevin has ever heard that a pastor did the first six months:* In one church I coached an executive pastor who was considered a great leader and knew how to lead the staff well and did so. A new senior pastor was hired. The new guy felt that he knew how to lead the staff better than the executive pastor, so he sidestepped him and undermined his authority. Today the senior pastor is gone and the executive pastor is now the senior pastor.

Pause and reflect question: Right now, without much thinking, what are some potential early wins in your new role that immediately come to mind? Why do you think they were top of the mind for you?

Next-step application: Carve out two hours this coming week to create your first draft six-month game plan. Don't try to make it perfect, but start somewhere.

CHAPTER 8

LEAD YOUR TEAM

Leadership is disappointing your own people at a rate they can absorb.
— Ronald Heifetz and Marty Linsky

Chapter snapshot:

Start early
Avoid common pitfalls
Define reality
Develop a six-month Game Plan
Lead your team
Establish trust

Successful onboarding requires that you lead your teams well. New leaders must invest in their leadership in seven ways, whether their teams are paid or volunteer. While this list does not comprehensively cover every leadership function, it's crucial to prioritize these decision areas your first six months: assessment, development, love, confrontation, challenge, emotional tone, and team fit.

Except in the rarest occasions, leadership was never meant to be done solo. You simply can't move your church or ministry forward by yourself. You need others to lean on, learn from, support you, and lead alongside you. Leadership expert Warren Bennis has said that behind every great leader is a great group. That implies that you must invest in your teams, whether they are paid staff or volunteers. During your first six months, this becomes especially critical. In fact, this step may impact your onboarding success more than any other factor.

Jim Collins, well-known leadership expert and author, studied over 1400 companies to discover what made a company great. Out of his research came the seminal book, *Good to Great: Why Some Companies Make the Leap… And Others Don't*. Many of the insights he discovered about business leadership also apply to church leadership. And he is credited with the phrase, "Get the right people on the bus." This insight, in particular, relates to this chapter's focus.

> *You are a bus driver. The bus, your company, is at a standstill, and it's your job to get it going. You have to decide where you're going, how you're going to get there, and who's going with you.*
>
> *Most people assume that great bus drivers (read: business leaders [and pastors]) immediately start the journey by announcing to the people on the bus where they're going—by setting a new direction or by articulating a fresh corporate vision.*
>
> *In fact, leaders of companies that go from good to great start not with "where" but with "who." They start by getting the right people on the bus, the wrong people off the bus, and the right people in the right seats. And they stick with that discipline—first the people, then the direction—no matter how dire the circumstances.*[109]

---

109 "Good to Great," Fast Company, September 30, 2001, http://www.fastcompany.com/43811/good-great.

If Collins is right, and I believe he is, what should you do to get the right people on the bus, the right people in the right seats, and the right people trained in the right way?

Although I wrote *Every Pastor's First 180 Days* as a guide for what leaders should do the first six months in a new ministry, it's not intended to be a comprehensive leadership book. Multiple authors have penned great books on the subject. However, in this chapter, I do suggest seven key leadership concepts that can help you lead your team well during those first six months, and beyond. You can download this self-evaluation tool∞ called *Seven Key Leadership Decisions*. I've excluded two essentials leadership qualities from this list that I've either covered before (*Listen and Learn*, chapter 2) or will cover (*Build Trust*, the next chapter).

As you read this chapter, it's crucial to initially clarify who your key teams are. During your first six months, squawkers and naysayers will tempt you to focus on them. Resist it. Invest your best time in leaders who can help move the ministry forward. In my case, our elder board and paid staff were my key teams. Although your team(s) may differ, clarify who they are.

Here are the seven decisions that will help you lead your team well:

1. Assess your team.

Start with this decision. Watkins recommends that you use the following criteria to assess your team.

- Competence. Does this person have the technical competence and experience to do the job effectively?
- Judgment. Does this person exercise good judgment, especially under pressure or when faced with making sacrifices for the greater good?
- Energy. Does this team member bring the right kind of energy to the job, or is she burned out or disengaged?
- Focus. Is this person capable of setting priorities and sticking to them, or prone to riding off in all directions?

- Relationships. Does this individual get along with others on the team and support collective decision-making, or is he difficult to work with?
- Trust. Can you trust this person to keep her word and follow through on commitments?[110]

To get answers to these questions, I've used three tools in my churches: a personality inventory, an emotional intelligence profile, and a staff self-evaluation tool. These three combined together can help you accurately assess your key staff and/or key volunteer leaders. Although a Google search will reveal many personality inventories, I recommend the *Leading from Your Strengths* inventory. For emotional intelligence (the ability to manage and be aware of our own and other's emotions), I use the inventory from the book *Emotional Intelligence 2.0* by Travis Bradberry. It includes a written key the purchaser can use to take an online assessment.[111] I created the third tool, *Staff Performance Review Self-Assessment,*∞ that I use for annual reviews. Rather than waiting a year for a review, I asked all the paid staff to take it shortly after I began my new ministry.

In addition to these tools, the six key questions I suggested in chapter 6 can also help you assess your team. I've included them again below for reference.

1. Tell me about yourself.
2. What's going well in your ministry and/or the church?
3. What is not going so well (ministry and/or the church) that you would like to see improved or addressed?
4. What burning question would you like to ask me?
5. If you were in my shoes what would you focus on?
6. How can I pray for you?

---

110 Watkins, *The First 90 Days*, Kindle e-book loc. 2372.

111 Travis Bradberry, Jean Greaves, and Patrick M. Lencioni, *Emotional Intelligence 2.0*, Har/Dol En edition (TalentSmart, 2009).

Ultimately, time, observation, and interaction will be your best teachers. If you combine what you learn from those three, your inventories, the six questions, and discerning prayer, you'll assess your team members accurately. When you do, you'll learn how to leverage their strengths and shore up their weaknesses. Team assessment will also help you fill holes in your team where weaknesses may exist.

Depending on your setting, you may have the liberty within those first six months to remove a staff person or volunteer who is not performing or who simply doesn't fit. In general, I suggest going slow in releasing any key leader unless someone on the team is toxic to the culture, blatantly disregards your leadership, or has committed serious moral or ethical sin.

2. Develop your team.

One key issue related to team development is this: *How will I do meetings?* When I arrived, the staff held their weekly meetings without an agenda, and our elder meetings would sometimes last over three hours. I quickly realized that to maximize our team meetings, I had to reformat them. Initially, I was the proverbial fly on the wall to observe how meetings were run. Here's how I handled my first few staff meetings.

Pre-meeting: I attended a staff meeting the week prior to my actual first day. I simply listened and communicated my excitement about being there. In this meeting, the elder chair attended to apologize to the staff for a decision the elders had made that had breached staff-elder trust. I responded with empathy and communicated that I wanted to build trust.

First meeting: I watched as the interim pastor led, whom I had asked to stay on for three months as part-time staff. In this meeting, I again affirmed the staff.

Second meeting: I asked the staff to complete the five statements exercise I explained in chapter 6, *Define Reality.* I also began to include a weekly calendar review of the church's upcoming events to keep us forward-looking.

Third meeting: I shared my big picture thoughts about what I hoped to accomplish the first six months, without being too specific. We began to use a written agenda (chapter 2 download). And I asked the staff to begin completing the short weekly report (see chapter 6).

Fourth meeting: I shared staff values (see below), and we did a small team building exercise. We asked a photographer to take a Christmas picture of the staff that we later mailed to the church. This provided a relational touch from the staff and a nice expression to the congregation.

Future meetings: From then on, I kept a similar agenda for each meeting. We shared what God had done the prior week. We prayed. Each staff person briefly shared their upcoming plans for the week. We reviewed the calendar. And we finished the meeting with some brief training and discussed big picture projects coming up. Throughout the meetings, I kept a positive tone and invited full participation from the staff.

For our twice-monthly elder meetings, which still went quite long, I suggested that we shorten them to two hours. We did this by limiting one monthly meeting to strategic issues and the next monthly meeting to tactical issues. As a result, we usually avoided unnecessarily long meetings and the board now felt that we were accomplishing significant tasks. We've now been able to pare those meetings to once a month.

A second issue to consider as you develop your team is, *How will I develop my team's skills?* I explain below what I did. Don't mimic my process but develop and implement a plan that works in your setting. Don't make it complicated, yet be intentional about it.

Within two months, I began to include a short leadership training component in our weekly staff meeting and periodically in our elders' meetings. Sometimes we'd watch a leadership video and discuss the content. Sometimes I'd assign a book or an article that we would read together and discuss. These training components added significant value to the team because they communicated that I cared about their leadership growth.

I also began a quarterly meeting we called Leadership Community. This meeting brings together all of our leaders at one time, when I train, cast vision, and build community. The volunteer leaders have responded well to this meeting for several reasons. As we communicate God's blessings on the church, their excitement has grown about their own ministries.

They feel honored because we provide nice refreshments. And they feel that these meetings add personal value to them because I always bring a strong leadership development lesson. In addition, I began an annual elders' retreat, a twice-annual staff retreat, and we now take many of our leaders to an annual leadership conference held in our city.

One final note. Some leadership experts suggest that you minimize team building until you can accurately assess who needs to stay on your team (or go). They recommend this to minimize relational fallout that could result if a well-liked leader is ultimately removed. You'll need to discern whether such advice applies to your setting.

3. Love your team.

The late Howard Hendricks, a beloved professor at Dallas Seminary, said that one of the most effective ways to motivate people is to intensify personal relationships. I've seen that principle prove true many times. As we build relational capital into the lives of others, relationships strengthen and become more resilient. Resilience gives leaders more capacity to endure interpersonal tension that inevitably rises in working relationships.

Leadership expert John Maxwell has also said, "People don't care how much you know until they know how much you care." Strong relationships help others respond more readily to your leadership. A key component of caring, empathy, is the ability to step into another person's shoes to see their experience through their eyes.

Psychologist Alfred Adler defined empathy as the ability to "to see with the eyes of another, to hear with the ears of another, to feel with the heart of another." When we communicate empathy to our teams, it builds depth and trust into your relationships with them. Empathy even prompts our brains to release the feel-good hormone oxytocin,[112] which results in a pragmatic benefit, as seen in one study of doctors. Empathetic doctors were

---

112   Jorge A. Barraza and Paul J. Zak, "Empathy toward Strangers Triggers Oxytocin Release and Subsequent Generosity," *Annals of the New York Academy of Sciences* 1167, no. 1 (June 1, 2009): 182–89, https://doi.org/10.1111/j.1749-6632.2009.04504.x.

sued less than those not considered empathetic.[113] So empathy can foster goodwill from your team toward you.

Another way to love your team is to help them manage stress. In chapter 1, *Prioritize Self and Family Care*, I listed four concepts that cause leadership stress: allostatic load, power stress, continuous partial attention, and multitasking. I also recommended four cures for leadership stress: exercise, statio, sleep, and getting off the grid. You can show your team you love them by teaching them these concepts and helping them monitor their own stress levels.

The Apostle Paul often modeled for us his deep love for others. He showed a special love for his young leadership protégé, Timothy. He spent time with him to train him. And he even used the endearing term, "son," to describe their relationship (1 Cor 4:15). Through this Paul provides us a great example of how we should love our fellow team members.

4. Confront your team.

To *confront your team* means that you don't avoid conflict and the hard conversations that often result. Jesus gave us a clear template to follow when difficulty or conflict requires tough conversations.

> *If your brother sins against you, go and show him his fault, just between the two of you. If he listens to you, you have won your brother over. But if he will not listen, take one or two others along, so that 'every matter may be established by the testimony of two or three witnesses.' If he refuses to listen to them, tell it to the church; and if he refuses to listen even to the church, treat him as you would a pagan or a tax collector."* (Matt 18:15-17 NIV)

When we avoid such conversations, the issue often comes back to bite us because the delay often makes things worse. Bradt, Check, and Pedraza

---

113 Nalini Ambady, "Surgeons' Tone of Voice: A Clue to Malpractice History" (Surgery, July 2002), http://www.communicationcache.com/uploads/1/0/8/8/10887248/ surgeons_tone_of_voice-_a_clue_to_malpractice_history.pdf.

wisely write, "Conflicts can freeze teams and cripple organizations. Groups almost inescapably have moments of internal conflict. A key sign of a leader is someone who can help the group handle its conflicts better. A leader helps people make sense of the conflict and see paths to resolution."[114]

Tense relationships will drain the life from you unless handled properly. Shortly after I arrived at WestPark, I realized that many in the church lacked good conflict resolution skills and, thus, avoided tough conversations. Some reverted to gossip instead. I noticed this among both lay leaders and some staff. As a result, I had to model and teach how we would handle conflict going forward.

Because I sensed that this issue was deeply rooted, as I wrote earlier, I devoted several sermons to conflict resolution during the first few months. At our second Leadership Community, I invited a guest speaker to speak on the topic. Our Solemn Assembly (see chapter 6) also helped pave the way toward healthy conflict resolution.

However, I had a few tough conversations in the first few months. One situation occurred when someone got angry about a conversation he had with another. Instead of talking one-on-one with the person to clear the air, he talked to someone else, who then sent a harsh email to every person on this particular team to let them know what happened. To correct the grapevine, I called the entire team together to clear the air. Fortunately, this decision stopped cold the misinformation and averted what could have been an early disaster.

In another situation, one staff person was not putting in full-time hours although he was a full-time employee. He was coming to work late and leaving early. I scheduled a meeting with him and gracefully explained my expectations. With this particular staff person, more tough conversations followed. He later realized he was not a good fit for the team.

I also had to confront a church member who publicly disrespected me. After I learned that she had done this for years with others, and been allowed

---

114   Bradt, Check, and Pedraza, *The New Leader's one hundred-Day Action Plan,* Kindle e-book loc. 5098.

to get away with it, I had a pointed conversation with her. I told her that such behavior would not be tolerated. Her behavior quickly changed for the better. Another church member was known for being gruff to people. I met with him and asked him to be kinder to others. He graciously heeded my advice, though he still needed some work.

I'm glad I didn't run from these conversations. They paid off. One elder even remarked two years later that he noticed that I was not afraid to have tough conversations. During your first six months, don't shy away from them but always be graceful when you have them.

5. Challenge your team.

As a leader, you want to bring out your team's best. That requires that you expect them to perform at their best. It's important to set a high bar, but not so high that you burn them or yourself out or create unrealistic expectations for them. One way to help your team perform well is through loving performance accountability. Healthy relationships certainly matter, but experts have discovered that relationships alone don't produce the highest employee engagement. Both relationship and performance expectations matter.[115]

Your staff and volunteers need to know what you expect of them, and they need feedback from you so they know if they're meeting your expectations. Sometimes getting feedback is as simple as asking, "How's the (such-and-such) project going?" Such a question provides real-time accountability and shows that you're interested in their ministry. You'll position your leaders for success with clear communication, feedback, and appreciation.

In the first few months, you'll want to evaluate your key staff member and/or volunteer leaders' job descriptions. If they don't exist, co-create them with each team member. You'll also want to help each staff member

---

115 Tomas Chamorro-Premuzic, "To Motivate Employees, Help Them Do Their Jobs Better," Harvard Business Review, November 12, 2014, https://hbr.org/2014/11/to-motivate-employees-help-them-do-their-jobs-better.

create goals for their respective ministries. Without clear job descriptions and clear goals, you have nothing against which to measure progress.

I also suggest that you establish staff and volunteer values, which often overlap. I define values as "shared assumptions about how we do things around here." Within sixty days, I shared what I call our *Permission to Play Values,*∞ the set of general guidelines I expected all the staff to embrace if they wanted to *play* on our team. They include qualities such as integrity, simplicity, good attitudes, teamwork, and authenticity. Every year I re-teach these to our staff and to our leadership community volunteers as well.

6. Set the emotional tone for your team.

Leaders possess a powerful subconscious tool called *emotional contagion.* It relates to certain kinds of brain cells called mirror neurons. Daniel Goleman, known for his work on emotional intelligence, says this: "Mirror neurons have particular importance in organizations, because leaders' emotions and actions prompt followers to mirror those feelings and deeds. The effects of activating neural circuitry in followers' brains can be very powerful."[116]

In other words, our actions, emotions, and demeanor (whether good or bad) are contagious, and our leaders will tend to mimic them. The Bible illustrates this principle in Proverbs 16:15: "There's life in the light of the king's face. His favor is like a cloud that brings spring rain" (NIV). In antiquity, when a subject saw a king smile at him, it communicated that the king's favor was on him. The result? The interaction would refresh the subject's spirit. He would "catch" the king's demeanor.

As a leader, you carry that same influence through your facial expression, tone of voice, body language, and actions. The emotional tone you set, whether good or bad, will ripple through your entire team. When you *ripple out* an uplifting mood or positive emotion, it will lift the spirits and performance of your entire team. So set a positive, Christlike tone every

---

116   Daniel Goleman and Richard Boyatzis, "Social Intelligence and the Biology of
     Leadership," *Harvard Business Review* 86, no. 9 (September 2008): 74–81, 136.

day in the office and every time you meet with your team members. They, in turn, will be more inclined to reflect it.

7. Determine who may not fit on your team.

Toward the end of your six months, you'll begin to see who may not be a good fit for your team. Unless you have a large staff and/or volunteer team or someone is being destructive to your team, you probably don't want to make leadership changes too soon. But, given time to assess performance, observe team dynamics, and build relationships, you may need to make some changes. Early on, begin asking yourself these questions about your team members:

- Are they a good fit in their current role?
- Are they an OK fit and need developing?
- Do you simply need more time to assess?
- Should you move him or her into another role or redefine their current role?
- Should they be replaced, but it's not critical to do so now?
- Do they need to be replaced, sooner than later?

Since the church had lost three staff members within a short period of time, and almost lost another, I decided to let a full year pass before I'd consider changing staff. But during the first year, I knew I had to evaluate which ones were keepers, which ones needed to go, and which ones I was unsure of. Almost all the staff proved to be keepers.

I did face an issue with one existing staff person. He was a delightful guy, but he just didn't seem to connect with me or my vision. He was candid about his feelings as was I with mine. I felt that at some point in the next few months, I would need to ask him to find another job in another ministry. I wanted to give him a chance to step up, though, and held a very candid meeting with him about my expectations. Shortly thereafter, he took another ministry opportunity that seemed to fit him well, and he left under good circumstances.

As you evaluate who needs to stay and who needs to potentially go, recognize that leaders who had endeared themselves to your predecessor may expect the same relationship with you. That may or may not happen. If it doesn't, don't be surprised if some opt out of leadership. As T. Scott Daniels writes, "There is no way you (can) replace the former relationship they had with the previous pastor or leader. Those losses are part of the natural ebb and flow of leadership transitions."[117]

Perhaps I should add one more quality to this list, build credibility. If you build into your team the other nine (seven here and the two I've covered elsewhere), credibility will follow. As I wrote this chapter, this quote reminded me what happens when we build credibility: *The great leader speaks little. He never speaks carelessly. He works without self-interest and leaves no trace. When all is finished, the people say, "We did it ourselves."*[118]

In this chapter, I've suggested seven essentials to help you *Lead your team.* However, one quality rises to a level that deserves an entire chapter. It's the "E" in the **SADDLE** strategy, *Establish Trust.*

———

Onboarding tips from an expert: Jenni Catron (www.jennicatron.com) is an author, the founder of the consulting group, The 4Sight Group, and the former executive pastor at Menlo Church in Menlo Park, California and Cross Point Church in Nashville, Tennessee

- *The best thing a new ministry leader/pastor can do during the first six months in a new church job:* The first six months for every leader should involve a lot of listening and learning. While you've likely done a great deal of homework about the church before accepting the job, there is still much to learn about the congregation, the staff team, and the culture. Be slow to action and more focused on building relationships, asking good questions, and learning about the community. You'll

---

117   Daniels, *The First 100 Days,* p. 149.

118   Bradt, Check, and Pedraza, *The New Leader's one hundred-Day Action Plan,* Kindle e-book locs. 382.

feel the urge to prove yourself with action, but you'll earn more trust and respect by building relationships first. From there you can determine the best next steps for leading forward.

- *The biggest mistake Jenny has ever seen a pastor do in the first six months:* Believe that he/she is the one who will turn the church or team around. I'm sure you've been hired to bring your experience and wisdom to this organization, but this can lead to the arrogant belief that you are the savior and as a result, you'll lack the humility to engage with a posture of learning. Find the value in what is there and then seek to bring your experience to build upon it. When you come in believing your ideas are the only way, you can create chaos that creates even more disruption.

Pause and reflect question: Which of the seven decisions makes you most uncomfortable as you think about implementing it? Why do you think that is so?

Next-step application: Take a few minutes and reflect on the decision that makes you most uncomfortable. How can you make yourself more comfortable with it? Here are some ideas: study Scripture that relates to it, ask a fellow pastor for his advice on how to get more comfortable with it, and commit to praying about this specific issue for seven straight days.

CHAPTER 9

ESTABLISH TRUST

Trust is a peculiar resource;
It is built rather than depleted by use.
— unknown

❧

Chapter snapshot:

Start early
Avoid common pitfalls
Define reality
Develop a six-month Game Plan
Lead your team
Establish trust

Trust in the church and in leadership is critical to move a ministry forward. Leaders must gauge the level of trust in their new ministry and then take specific action to build trust. In this chapter, I include a trust inventory to assess the trust level and suggest eight practical ways that help leaders grow trust.

As I shared in chapter 6 on *Define Reality*, I recognized several burning issues WestPark faced. One of them, a lack of trust, loomed large. I sensed a lack of trust between staff and elders, between elders and the church, and between the church and the staff. Since I felt that this issue lay at the root of some of the other challenges, I made trust-building a key component of my six-month game plan.

I believe it's so important for every new pastor's onboarding success that I've devoted this entire chapter to it. A new leader may bring strong competencies in preaching, strategic planning, and vision casting and may carry a significant title, but without trust, few will succeed in the first six months, or beyond. Title and competencies don't automatically confer trust. Here's what others have said about trust and leadership.

Trust is quite possibly the single most powerful influential lever for leaders and organizations today.[119]

> – Stephen M. R. Covey, author of *The Speed of Trust* and
> *the son of the late Stephen Covey*

The irreducible minimum in leadership is trust.[120]

> – Jim Osterhaus of TAG church consulting

Being seen as someone who can be trusted, who has high integrity, and who is honest and truthful is essential.[121]

> – James Kouzes and Barry Posner,
> well-known leadership experts and authors

---

119 Covey, Stephen M.R., "Trust Is a Competency," *Chief Learning Officer* 7, no. 5 (May 2008), https://www.chieflearningofficer.com/2008/04/29/trust-is-a-competency/.

120 Tod Bolsinger, *Canoeing the Mountains: Christian Leadership in Uncharted Territory* (Downers Grove, IL: IVP Books, 2015), Kindle e-book loc. 991.

121 James M. Kouzes and Barry Z. Posner, *Credibility: How Leaders Gain and Lose It, Why People Demand It*, 2 edition (San Francisco, Calif: Jossey-Bass, 2011), p. 24.

Trust is the ultimate intangible. It has no shape or substance, yet it empowers our actions. And its presence or absence can govern our behavior as if it were a tangible force. . . . Trust is the 'miracle ingredient' in organizational life (church life, my notation)—a lubricant that reduces friction, a bonding agent that glues together disparate parts, a catalyst that facilitates action. No substitute —neither threat nor promise —will do the job as well."[122]

– Gordon Shea, author

Unfortunately, in today's world, trust in leadership is lacking. Each year the Edelman company takes a worldwide survey to gauge trust. Called the Edelman Trust Barometer, it asks respondents how well they trust four organizations to do the right thing, and by extension, their leaders. The results show that in 2018, 47 percent trust the government, 47 percent trust the media, 56 percent trust business, and only 56 percent trust NGO's, which would include churches.[123] And in another statistic, only 46 percent of disengaged employees trust their leaders, whereas 96 percent of engaged employees trust their leaders.[124] Another study in 2013 examined how well the American public esteemed various professions. Pastors came in sixth place, with only 37 percent of the respondents stating that they believe pastors contribute a lot to society's well-being. The military, teachers, medical doctors, scientists, and engineers were viewed more favorably.

Trust is built, not necessarily conferred because you are the new guy. Trust is like a piggy bank, and every leader has a piggy bank trust account. You can only drop one coin at a time into a ceramic piggy bank, much like how you build trust, incrementally. If you remove the plug in the bottom

---

122   Gordon F. Shea, *Building Trust in the Workplace*, First Printing edition (New York, N.Y: AMA Membership Publications, 1984), p. 54.

123   "Edelman - Communications Marketing Firm," Edelman, accessed May 21, 2019, https://www.edelman.com/sites/g/files/aatuss191/files/2019-02/2019_Edelman_Trust_Barometer_Global_Report_2.pdf .

124   Covey, *"Trust Is a Competency."*

of the bank, you can quickly empty it of its coins. Likewise, you can quickly lose trust. Building trust is slow yet losing it is fast, and re-building it comes even more slowly. Whether your new ministry has a void of trust as did my new church, I encourage you to prioritize trust building during your onboarding period.

From a biblical perspective, the word trust, trusted, or trustworthy appears over 171 times in the Bible. Most of the verses refer to the vertical dimension, our need to trust God. But I believe that building our trust account with others parallels our trust relationship with God. The more we truly trust Jesus, the more He becomes our security and significance. As a result, we can risk trusting others and open ourselves to them trusting us. As we learn to trust God more, we can trust others more and they can trust us more.

We must build trust around a core, foundational trust in Jesus and a secondary trust in others and ourselves. Trust in others is based on trusting the Lord. And Scripture says much about trust.

- *Trust in the LORD with all your heart and lean not on your own understanding.* (Prov 3:5 NIV)
- *... those who are trustworthy can keep a confidence.* (Prov 11:13 NIV)
- *Like the coolness of snow at harvest time is a trustworthy messenger to those who send him; he refreshes the spirit of his masters.* (Prov 25:13 NIV)
- *When I am afraid, I will trust in you.* (Ps 56:3 NIV)
- *But blessed is the man who trusts in the LORD, whose confidence is in him.* (Jer 17:1 NIV)
- *Do not let your hearts be troubled. Trust in God; trust also in me.* (John 14:1 NIV)
- *May the God of hope fill you with all joy and peace as you trust in him, so that you may overflow with hope by the power of the Holy Spirit.* (Rom 15:13 NIV)

People who struggle to trust often do so because trust has been broken often in their other relationships. And they may fill your new ministry. Your church may even face a strong deficit of trust, as I experienced at WestPark. If so, acknowledge that fact and rebuild the trust level.

From a neurochemistry perspective, trust fosters even more trust because it causes the brain to release what is called the trust hormone, oxytocin.[125] When we feel safe with others, this brain chemical engenders feelings of warmth, belonging, and security. Because it feels good, we want more of it. Thus, trust fosters more trust. In contrast, when we are not with those we trust or when trust has been broken, our brains assume a posture of distrust and the stress hormone, cortisol, releases.

We need cortisol when we face good stress because it motivates and energizes us and heightens our ability to deal with danger. But when cortisol remains high for extended periods of time, which happens under chronic stress, it damages our hearts and impairs mental functioning and memory.[126] It also diminishes teamwork and can fray relationships because people are more on edge and can be more defensive.

Some families and churches are awash in cortisol and sorely lack oxytocin. The atmosphere is filled with distrust. I call this a cortisol culture.

What might a cortisol culture that diminishes trust look and feel like? Here are five indicators of such a culture:

1. People relate to each other in a guarded, suspicious way, always on guard to protect themselves if need be. They are fearful of what might happen if they become vulnerable, so they stay closed to others and keep their cards close to their chests.

2. It is filled with excessive and cumbersome policies, procedures, and bylaws. For if you don't trust others to make good decisions

125 Michael Kosfeld et al., "Oxytocin Increases Trust in Humans," *Nature* 435, no. 7042 (June 2, 2005): 673–76, https://doi.org/10.1038/nature03701.

126 Madhumita Murgia, *How Stress Affects Your Brain*, https://ed.ted.com/lessons/how-stress-affects-your-brain-madhumita-murgia#review.

or assume ill motive in them, you have to make sure you cover all the contingencies. You do that by writing everything down. Rules govern that culture rather than trusting relationships. Excessive analysis often leads to paralysis.

3. People assume questionable motives from others, make wrong assumptions, and impute ill intent. They think they know what others are thinking and automatically assume it's not good. They connect dots and create fearful scenarios when none really exist. They assume the worst.

4. Little grace or allowances for failure exists. A "one strike and you're out" atmosphere prevails. As a result, people often avoid reasonable risks and steps of faith because they don't want to get reprimanded.

5. Fear abounds.

As you begin your first six months, determine if a lack of trust is affecting your team or church. In addition to the above indicators, these questions might provide clues if a trust deficit exists. You can download the *Trust Evaluation Tool*∞ to help you gauge your ministry's trust level.

1. Is a spirit of suspicion evident in how team members relate to each other?
2. Do team members overly rely on email in lieu of talking?
3. Do team members seem to wear facades?
4. Does there seem to be too much "happy talk," which may mask true problems?
5. Are team members reluctant to share their honest feelings and opinions?
6. Do team members resist meeting together?
7. Has the team lost enthusiasm?
8. Is grumbling and complaining the norm?
9. Are current leaders inconsistent in their leadership and life in Christ?
10. Do some team members intentionally withhold information from others?

Even if your church does not reflect a cortisol culture, I still encourage you to build into your six-month plan ways to build trust. You will need to build trust even in a healthy environment. Below I suggest eight ways to add to your trust piggy bank and related scriptures. You can download the *Eight Ways to Build Trust* tool.∞

1. Lead with integrity in everything you do.

Integrity involves not only your own private world but also how you treat others. Be fair with others. Don't play favorites. Treat your critics with respect. Build your moral compass around Jesus. Never cut moral corners. The biblical character Daniel refused to compromise his convictions even though it put him in difficult situations. Your team will respect you if you live a life of integrity. Remember that Satan will try to trip you. He wants you to fail, but Jesus wants you to succeed.

But the noble man makes noble plans, and by noble deeds he stands. (Isa 32:8 NIV)

2. Speak truth, but always in love.

Don't spin and don't flatter. Tell the truth, but don't wield it like a bat. Jim Carrey starred in a movie several years ago called *Liar Liar.* He always spoke the truth but with no love, consideration, or respect.

As I wrote in the prior chapter, leaders must never evade tough conversations. Patrick Lencioni, well-known leadership consultant and author, wrote, "Trust is knowing that when a team member does push you, they're doing it because they care about the team."[127]

One of the most successful ways to deplete your trust piggy bank is to send angry emails. Never send an angry email. It's always best to have tough conversations face-to-face.

Instead, speaking the truth in love, we will in all things grow up into him who is the Head, that is, Christ. (Eph 4:15 NIV)

---

127 Patrick Lencioni, *The Five Dysfunctions of a Team: A Leadership Fable*, 1st edition (San Francisco: Jossey-Bass, 2002), Kindle e-book loc. 1841.

3. *Golden rule* trust.

If you extend trust to others, they will give it back to you. If you don't trust others, don't expect them to trust you. Trust gets reciprocated. If you want trust, you must give trust.

Biblically rooted trust does not mean blind trust. Stephen M. R. Covey calls healthy trust, *smart trust*. You must see at least some credibility and history in another before you offer him or her full trust. Smart trust means that you have a propensity to trust and that you extend and inspire trust in others.

Do to others whatever you would like them to do to you. (Matt 7:12 NIV)

4. Risk transparency.

People don't trust what they don't see. Trust requires humility. And humility often means that you become vulnerable to others. When you do, you give others the power to potentially hurt or disappoint you. Trust comes when you take such risks. Be willing to admit your struggles. Your team wants to see strength in you, but also vulnerability.

But we have this treasure in jars of clay to show that this all-surpassing power is from God and not from us. (2 Cor 4:7 NIV)

5. Go the extra mile to right wrongs.

Don't cover up. Don't make excuses. Own your own failures. Sincerely apologize and make restitution when necessary. Don't blame others for your mistakes and failures. You will fail at times, and when you do, your team will watch to see how you respond. They don't expect perfection, but they expect that you will right your wrongs.

If someone forces you to go one mile, go with him two miles. (Matt 5:41 NIV)

6. Only gossip good.

Speak about others as if they were present. If your team hears you gossip or speak ill of another person, it will erode trust. We all subconsciously (or consciously) think that if someone gossips in front of us, it will only be a matter of time before we are the topic of their gossip with someone else. Only speak well of others in the presence of your team. Give others credit, and never take credit for their successes.

Do not let any unwholesome talk come out of your mouths, but only what is helpful for building others up according to their needs, that it may benefit those who listen. (Eph 4:29 NIV)

7. Do what you say you are going to do.

Often pastors think of integrity only in terms of character. That is, a good leader should be trusted if he loves God, loves his family, and doesn't commit a lot of sins. Character is an important component of trust, but competency also matters. Character is like the roots of a tree below ground and competency is like the part of the tree above ground—its branches, leaves, and fruit. Competency means not only that you can be counted on to do what you say you'll do but that your track record shows you can be trusted.

People want to see that you follow through on your plans and intentions. They want to see progress. Lead your ministry forward. Show results. Early wins will build trust. Don't be all talk and no action. Be good at what you do. Hold yourself accountable and responsible. Don't blame others when you should take responsibility. Few things will build trust as quickly as tangible results.

Now it is required that those who have been given a trust must prove faithful. (1 Cor 4:2 NIV)
"Well done, my good servant!" his master replied. "Because you have been trustworthy in a very small matter, take charge of ten cities." (Luke 19:17 NIV)

8. Seek understanding before being understood.

Stephen Covey is credited with this phrase. It means to truly listen. I've devoted an entire chapter (chapter 2) to listening and learning. Here I expand that to apply to your team. The better you know your team, the more you'll understand why they do what they do. And listening to them is the best way to understand them. When your team feels listened to, the more you will convey empathy. And when you empathize, you build trust.[128]

My dear brothers, take note of this: Everyone should be quick to listen, slow to speak and slow to become angry.... (James 1:19 NIV)

One final thought. A few weeks after I started at WestPark, I shared an illustration to convey my commitment to them for the long haul. I brought a large empty jar and a similar large jar only filled with over 520 green marbles. I said that the jar with marbles stood for ten years of weeks, each marble representing a week. I told the church that I hoped the Lord would allow me to stay at least ten years. I explained that this not only reminded me of my commitment to them but helped me keep each week in perspective.

I explained that each week I would move one marble from the full jar to the empty jar. I wanted these jars to visually remind me of my long-term commitment to them and to remind me to not allow one bad week to negatively affect me. Two-and-a-half years later, one of the elders emailed this to me: *Your marble jar was a brilliant way to demonstrate to a congregation that had seen a large number of staff and pastoral changes that you planned to be here for a good period of time.* Unintentionally, that illustration helped the church and my team build trust in me. Perhaps a similar visual can do the same for you.

In this chapter, I've unpacked the final concept, the "E," in the **SADDLE** strategy, *Establish Trust.* So where do you go from here? I cover that in the next chapter as I show you how to implement the **PALM** and the **SADDLE** strategy.

———

———

128   "The Neuroscience of Trust," Psychology Today, accessed May 22, 2019, https://www.psychologytoday.com/blog/the-athletes-way/201508/the-neuroscience-trust.

Onboarding tips from an expert: Lance Witt, former Executive Pastor, Saddleback Church, California and founder of Replenish, a church/ leadership consulting organization geared to help leaders lead out of a healthy soul (www.replenish.net)

- *The best thing a new pastoral ministry leader can do during the first six months:* I always tell new pastors to adopt the Triple-L strategy in the first six months... Love, Learn, and Listen.
- *The dumbest thing Lance has ever heard that a pastor did the first six months:* Trying to change the name of the church.

Pause and reflect question: How would you rate your ability to trust others?

Next-step application: Take one of the eight trust building suggestions and intentionally apply it this coming week as you relate to your team.

CHAPTER 10

PULLING IT ALL TOGETHER

The secret to getting ahead is getting started.
— Mark Twain

⌁

Chapter snapshot:

In this chapter, I wrap things up. I list each template by chapter for easy reference, suggest key tasks to accomplish before your first day on the job, explain how the twenty-six-week Weekly Check-In exercises work,∞ and offer a final challenge.

As we come to the end, I hope you've learned enough about onboarding to prompt you to apply these concepts in your new role. With the *PALM* acronym, I laid the foundation for successful onboarding with four key principles.

- **P**rioritize self and family care.
- **A**vidly overcommunicate.
- **L**isten and learn.
- **M**anage change wisely.

These four principles provide a lens through which to apply the insights from the six-step *SADDLE* process.

- **S**tart early.
- **A**void common pitfalls.
- **D**efine reality.
- **D**evelop a game plan.
- **L**ead your team.
- **E**stablish trust.

However, since I've covered so much material, you may be thinking, "How can I apply everything given the other ministry demands I'll face in my new role?" If you feel that way, I hope this chapter will allay your concerns. What follows is a systematic process to apply these onboarding principles without feeling overwhelmed. However, it will take your commitment to set aside time before you begin and during the first six months to progressively build and execute your onboarding plan. My suggestions fall into two timeframes: the weeks leading up to your hiring/move/day one on the job and during your first six months on the job.

In this final chapter, I will help you organize your plan in three ways. First, below I list all the downloadable tools∞ corresponding to the chapter where I mentioned them. Second, I suggest how you can maximize your preparation during the weeks leading up to your first day on the job. Third, I explain how the twenty-six-week *Weekly Check-in Template* works.∞

The downloadable∞ templates, guides, and inventories listed by chapter

- **Chapter 1**
  - **Burnout Inventory**: a simple inventory to help you determine the level of personal burnout in your life, important to discern before you begin.
  - **Safe Friends Checklist**: a comprehensive list of qualities to look for in a safe friend.

- **Chapter 2**
  - **Ninety-Day Progress Report**: an example of a report I gave to the church after ninety days.
  - **Communications Template**: helps you align what you need to communicate with the venues available for communication at your new church.
  - **Staff Meeting Agenda Template**: a suggested agenda template to use in staff meetings.

- **Chapter 3**
  - **Change Management Checklist**: helps you think about issues that affect change as you plan change initiatives.

- **Chapter 4**
  - **True North Values example**: an example (mine) of what your true north values might look like.
  - **How to Discover Your True North Values Retreat Plan**: provides guidelines for a personal retreat to discern your true north values.
  - **Know Yourself Matrix**: maps out who you are so that you can make the wisest decision about a potential new job and relate well with others in that new job, all based on how God has wired you.
  - **Guiding Principles**: defines how a board and a lead pastor might relate to each other.
  - **Key Hiring Questions**: provides key hiring questions to ask at different time frames during the hiring process.
  - **Miscellaneous Hiring Questions**: provides additional questions that might be helpful in the hiring process.

- **Chapter 5**
  - **Pitfalls Checklist**: lists the seven common pitfalls a new pastor can fall into.

- **Chapter 6**
  - **Key Staff/Volunteer/Stakeholder Questions**: provides three lists of key questions/statements to be completed based on your audience (staff, volunteers, key stakeholders).
  - **Appreciative Inquiry (AI)**: a step-by-step guide for leading an appreciative inquiry with your key leaders; AI is a unique brainstorming session that focuses on positives and future opportunities rather than on problems and the past.
  - **Cultural Discernment Questions**: questions that can help you discern your new ministry's culture.
  - **SWOT Analysis Example**: helps you visually see your church's strengths and weakness (my church's SWOT).

- **Chapter 7**
  - **Begin with the End in Mind Template**: helps you begin to think about what you hope to accomplish the first six months in your new job.
  - **Six-Month Game Plan Example**: expands on the *Begin with the End in Mind Template* above; helps you flesh out your six-month plan.
  - **Dashboard Example**: helps you visually place your ministry's mission/vision, values, objectives, and goals in a simple, easy-to-view document.
  - **Personal and Ministry Mission Statement Example**: illustrates what a personal mission and ministry statement might look like (my mission statement).

- **Chapter 8**
  - **Seven Key Leadership Decisions**: helps you evaluate yourself on the seven key leadership decisions you should make during your first six months.
  - **Permission to Play Values**: illustrates core values you should expect staff and key volunteers to adhere to.

- **Staff Performance Self-Assessment**: a template for a natural, effective way to perform staff reviews.

- **Chapter 9**
  - **Eight Ways to Build Trust**: includes the eight ways to build trust with your team.
  - **Trust Evaluation Tool**: helps you gauge the level of trust or mistrust in your new ministry.

- **Chapter 10**
  - **Twenty-Six-Week Weekly Check-in Template**: provides twenty-six weekly onboarding exercises that include key questions, a key principle to review, suggested tools, and prompts about next steps you might want to take.

What to Do During Your Pre-Hiring/Pre-Move Bonus Weeks

View the weeks prior to your hire/first day as bonus weeks, valuable time to get ahead. Hiring visits, leaving your current ministry well, preparing for the physical move, and the move itself will take significant time and energy. However, I can't overestimate the value of being prepared before day one. After you're hired, try to negotiate as much time between leaving your current job and starting your new one as is financially feasible. I had the luxury of three weeks between moving and my first day at WestPark. In retrospect, I could have used an extra week. During those bonus weeks, I suggest scheduling at least two entire days or four half-days to work through these critical tasks.

1. Carefully read or re-read the book.
2. Download and print all the templates and place them in a notebook for easy reference.
3. After you've downloaded and printed the *Weekly Check-in Template*, date each of the first twenty-six weeks corresponding to the weeks of your first six months.

4. In addition to the time you spend before you make your move, schedule two thirty-minute appointments with yourself each week beginning the first week on the job, one at the beginning of the week (a weekly preview to plan ahead) and one at the end of each week (a weekly review to evaluate what happened). During your first six months, these sessions are crucial. Don't let other demands crowd them out.

5. Spend significant time on the content in chapter 4, *Start Early*. Although each week on the job you'll ask yourself what you can do to get a head start for that week, the weeks prior to your first day on the job provide significant opportunity to prepare yourself to get ahead. Ideally, you will come into your job with these tasks completed:

   • A thorough pre-hiring process that maximized understanding of your new role and what will be expected of you (refer to these downloads: *Miscellaneous Hiring Questions* and *Key Hiring Questions*).

   • Clarity on your true north values (refer to these downloads: *True North Values Example* and the *How to Discover Your True North Values Retreat Plan*). I encourage you to take a personal overnight retreat to work through this material to clarify your true north values.

   • A good understanding of your gifts, strengths, and personality styles (refer to this download: *Know Yourself Matrix*). Consider taking some of the assessments recommended in this tool before day one.

6. Begin dreaming about what you hope to accomplish your first six months on the job. Remember, you still have much to learn before you create a concrete six-month game plan. But based on what you know, it's helpful to begin prayerfully collecting your thoughts and ideas before you arrive (refer to chapter 7 and these templates: *Begin with the End in Mind* and *Six-Month Game Plan Example*).

7. Craft a clear personal mission statement. A personal mission statement, along with your *True North Values* and your *Know Yourself Matrix,* comprises your ministry compass to keep you on track when demands outstrip your available time and energy. They will help you serve from your God-given calling and strengths and know what to say *yes* and *no* to (refer to chapter 7 and the download, *Personal Mission Statement Example*).

What to Do Each Week During the First Six Months to Enhance Your Onboarding

I suggested above that you download and print the *Weekly Check-in Template*. This template provides twenty-six short weekly check-ins to help keep the concepts fresh and to help you apply them during your six-month onboarding period. You'll spend thirty minutes at the beginning of each week to preview and plan what you need to focus on for that week. Then, at the end of the week, you'll spend another thirty minutes reviewing what you learned. I've included a generic weekly check-in below to give you an idea what each week looks like. Essentially, in each of these thirty-minute planning periods, you'll pray, ask questions related to the PALM principles and the SADDLE process, and then record your plans, tasks, necessary appointments, and learnings. During your beginning-of-week sessions, you will ask the questions prospectively, that is, with the coming week in mind (i.e., How *will* I prioritize self and family?). During your end-of-week sessions, you will ask the same questions retrospectively, that is, in review of the week that just passed (i.e., How well *did* I prioritize self and family?). Here's a generic look at what the twenty-six weekly check-ins look like in the *Weekly Check-in Template*.

WEEK 1 (date – i.e., Jan. 1–7)

1. Pray: *Prepare your heart, ask the Lord to bless your onboarding plan, and seek His wisdom for the upcoming week.*

2. Preview (thirty-minute beginning-of-week session): *With the coming week in mind, ask yourself these questions about each concept:*

- *PALM* principles
    - **P**: How will I *prioritize self and family* this week?
    - **A**: What is the main message I need to *avidly communicate* and how can I best do that?
    - **L**: How can I *listen and learn* better?
    - **M**: How can I most effectively *manage change?*

- *SADDLE* process
    - **S**: What do I need to *start early*/get a head start on this week?
    - **A**: How can I *avoid pitfalls* and which ones do I need to be especially careful to avoid?
    - **D**: What do I need to do to *define reality* more clearly?
    - **D**: What do I need to do to *develop my game plan* more fully?
    - **L**: What can I do to *lead my team* better?
    - **E**: How can I *establish trust* more effectively with my team and the church?
- Helpful concept to review: (changes each week)
- Applicable template/chapter: (varies)

3. Review (thirty-minute end-of-week session): *Ask the same questions retrospectively.* (i.e., How well *did I* prioritize self and family?)

4. Record: *Record to-dos, appointments, and insights.*

> Three tasks I must do/when I will do them. Transfer these to your personal calendar and the task management program/to-do list you use.
> 1.
> 2.
> 3.
> Insights I learned in my end-of-week review. Record them in a journal if that works best for you.

In addition to my twice weekly check-ins, two other practices helped me onboard successfully. First, I kept a weekly journal that helped me sort through difficult and frustrating emotions. The simple act of writing down our negative emotions enhances our emotional health.[129] I did that and it helped me track my progress. Second, as I explained in chapter 7, I also scheduled a larger block of time each week for more in-depth strategic planning. I seldom skipped it. It was a lifesaver, as it helped me plan well my very busy weeks.

***

As I conclude, I don't want to imply that I did everything right. However, I did do several things right. My first six months paved the way for a very satisfying experience partly because I consistently applied these onboarding principles. But in retrospect, if I could rewind my first year, I would have placed less pressure on myself, slowed my pace, taken more time to reflect, and worried less. In a new job, it is easy to run at an unhealthy pace.

As you prepare for a new ministry role, I leave you with these final thoughts. Remember that you won't have only one six-month season in your church. You will have many new six-month seasons in the same church. Consider building these onboarding principles into the fabric of your leadership. As you apply them and see God's blessing, pause long enough to celebrate the wins He gives you.

Adjust to inevitable surprises you will face. You could spend eight hours each day on your onboarding plan and still be blindsided with unexpected conflict, crises, and misunderstanding. When that happens, lean deeply into your relationship with Jesus. There is a reason we call Him our Rock. King David often faced challenges to his leadership. He describes

---

129   Karen A. Baikie and Kay Wilhelm, "Emotional and Physical Health Benefits of Expressive Writing," *Advances in Psychiatric Treatment* 11, no. 5 (September 1, 2005): 338–46, https://doi.org/10.1192/apt.11.5.338.

God's strength through several strong metaphors in Psalm 18:2: *The LORD is my rock, my fortress and my deliverer; my God is my rock, in whom I take refuge. He is my shield and the horn of my salvation, my stronghold.*

Finally, as you seek to make a Kingdom difference for God, remember and heed the words of the Apostle Paul in 1 Corinthians 15:58:

> *Therefore, my dear brothers, stand firm. Let nothing move you.*
> *Always give yourselves fully to the work of the Lord, because you know*
> *that your labor in the Lord is not in vain.*